Evidentiality in Japanese

Hituzi Linguistics in English

No. 16 *Derivational Linearization at the Syntax-Prosody Interface*   Kayono Shiobara
No. 17 *Polysemy and Compositionality*   Tatsuya Isono
No. 18 *fMRI Study of Japanese Phrasal Segmentation*   Hideki Oshima
No. 19 *Typological Studies on Languages in Thailand and Japan*   Tadao Miyamoto et al.
No. 20 *Repetition, Regularity, Redundancy*   Yasuyo Moriya
No. 21 *A Cognitive Pragmatic Analysis of Nominal Tautologies*   Naoko Yamamoto
No. 22 *A Contrastive Study of Responsibility for Understanding Utterances between Japanese and Korean*   Sumi Yoon
No. 23 *On Peripheries*   Anna Cardinaletti et al.
No. 24 *Metaphor of Emotions in English*   Ayako Omori
No. 25 *A Comparative Study of Compound Words*   Makiko Mukai
No. 26 *Grammatical Variation of Pronouns in Nineteenth-Century English Novels*   Masami Nakayama
No. 27 *I mean as a Marker of Intersubjective Adjustment*   Takashi Kobayashi
No. 28 *Lexical Pragmatics*   Akihiko Kawamura
No. 29 *An Affect-Oriented English Pronunciation Instructional Design for Japanese University Students*   Junko Chujo
No. 30 *The Diffusion of Western Loanwords in Contemporary Japanese*   Aimi Kuya
No. 31 *Tag Questions and Their Intersubjectivity*   Hiromi Nakatani
No. 32 *Biliteracy in Young Japanese Siblings*   Joy Taniguchi
No. 33 *The Pragmatics of Clausal Conjunction*   Miyuki Nagatsuji
No. 34 *A Cognitive Linguistic Approach to Japanese Agrammatism*   Hiroko Ihara
No. 35 *English Prepositions in Usage Contexts*   Fumino Horiuchi
No. 36 *Integrated Skills Development*   Takayuki Nakamori
No. 37 *Perception and Linguistic Form*   Kiyomi Tokuyama
No. 38 *The No More A than B Construction*   Atsushi Hirota
No. 39 *A Contrastive Study of Function in Intonation Systems*   Ken-ichi Kadooka
No. 40 *Evidentiality in Japanese*   Akira Takashima

Hituzi Linguistics in English

40

AKIRA TAKASHIMA

—

Evidentiality in Japanese

—

A Cognitive Linguistic Approach to the Evidential Marker *-rasi-i*

HITUZI
SYOBO

Copyright © Akira Takashima 2025
First published 2025

Author: Akira Takashima

All rights reserved. Except for the quotation of short passages for the purposes of criticism and review, no part of this publication may be reproduced, stored in a retrieval system, or transmitted in any form or by any means, electronic, mechanical, photocopying, recording or otherwise, without the written prior permission of the publisher.

In case of photocopying, electronic copying, and retrieval from the network for personal use, permission will be given upon receipt of payment and approval from the publisher. For details please contact us through e-mail. Our e-mail address is given below.

Hituzi Syobo Publishing

Yamato bldg. 2f, 2-1-2 Sengoku
 Bunkyo-ku Tokyo, Japan 112-0011
Telephone: +81-3-5319-4916
Facsimile: +81-3-5319-4917
e-mail: toiawase@hituzi.co.jp
https://www.hituzi.co.jp/
postal transfer: 00120-8-142852

ISBN978-4-8234-1278-3
Printed in Japan

Acknowledgments

The main body of this book is an expansion and enhancement of my doctoral dissertation submitted to Kanazawa University in 2021. I would like to express my deepest appreciation to all those who provided assistance throughout the preparation of this book.

First of all, I would like to express my sincere thanks to Professor Yuko Horita, my supervisor. Her warm words of encouragement and invaluable comments for my research helped me a lot. Her insightful advice led me deep into the study of Linguistics and helped me clarify my ideas. I would also like to thank Professor Tomoaki Takayama and Professor Koji Irie for their useful comments and constructive suggestions. Without their advice and support, this study would not have been possible.

I would also like to express my special gratitude to Professor Yoshihisa Nakamura, who encouraged me to pursue my research interest and offered valuable advice. And I am grateful to Professor Hideto Hamada, who led me to aspire to an academic career.

I am also grateful to professors Tetsuo Nitta and Yoshikata Shibuya at Kanazawa University for their insightful comments and continuous support. I have benefited from discussions with the following alumni and current students at the graduate school of Kanazawa University: Li Qu, Yoshimi Kawabata, Mizue Tanaka, Takashi Kobayashi, Hiromi Nakatani, Rie Mukai, Atsushi Hirota, Miki Yamada, Keiichi Ishigaki, and Yusho Arai. Advice and comments given by Yasuhiro Tsushima at Fuji Women's University and Shotaro Sasaki at Kochi University have been a great help in my study as well. I also thank Miki Yamada, who took time to help reviewing my English in this book. I would like also to thank Dane Hampton for reviewing my English language and giving generous support and input as a native speaker of English.

Finally, a special word of thanks to my parents, Yasunori and Masako, who have helped me with their love and heartfelt support in numerous ways throughout my graduate studies.

This work was supported by grant-in-aid for publication of scientific research results from the president of Onomichi City University.

Contents

Acknowledgments		V
Abbreviations		XI
List of Figures		XIII
List of Tables		XV

CHAPTER 1
Introduction

1

CHAPTER 2
Evidentiality

2.1.	Introduction	5
2.2.	The parameters of evidentiality and how they are marked	6
2.3.	Evidentiality in Japanese	14
2.4.	Where do evidentialities come from?	21
2.5.	Epistemic modality vs. evidentiality	23
2.5.1.	Palmer (1986)	23
2.5.2.	Van der Auwera and Plugian (1998)	24
2.5.3.	De Haan (2001)	26
2.5.4.	The relation between modality and evidentiality: from the study of cognitive linguistics	27
2.6.	Mirativity	29
2.7.	What is at issue?	32

CHAPTER 3
The concept of subjectivity in
cognitive grammar

3.1.	Introduction	35

3.2.	Subjectification	37
3.3.	Grounding and layering	39
3.4.	De-subjectification	44
3.5.	The cycle of awakening	48
3.6.	Summary	51

CHAPTER 4
The language change of
Japanese evidential *-rasi-i*

4.1.	Introduction	53
4.2.	Previous research on *-rasi-i*	54
4.2.1.	The relationship between inference and hearsay: Kida (2013)	57
4.2.2.	The relationship between suffixal and evidential *-rasi-i*: Miyake (2006)	59
4.2.3.	What is at issue?	61
4.3.	Grammaticalization	64
4.3.1.	Unidirectionality: grammaticalization as reduction and expansion	67
4.4.	The emergence of Japanese evidentialities	72
4.4.1.	The historical transition of *-gena* and *-sauna* (*-soo=da*): Senba (1972)	72
4.4.2.	The historical transition of *-rasi-i*	76
4.5.	The transition from the early years of the Modern Era to the Modern Era	81
4.6.	The language change of the evidential *-rasi-i*: subjectification and de-subjectification	87
4.6.1.	Language change from the suffixal usage to the evidential usage	87
4.6.2.	The emergence of the hearsay parameter from the inference parameter	92

CHAPTER 5
How evidentiality is expressed in novels

5.1.	Introduction	97
5.2.	Cognitive linguistics and narratology	98
5.2.1.	The narrator and focalizer in the framework of	

	narratology	99
5.2.2.	Fashion of construal: the two types of construal	101
5.3.	Comparing evidential -*rasi-i* in Japanese with its counterparts in English	103
5.4.	The difference in the encoding of evidential meanings between Japanese and English	106
5.5.	The cognitive factor reflected in the different markedness of evidentiality	110

CHAPTER 6

The extension of meaning into mirativity
in the Japanese evidential marker -*rasi-i*

6.1.	Introduction	113
6.2.	Evidentiality from the perspective of the theory of territory	114
6.3.	Mirativity as a general cognitive phenomenon	117
6.3.1.	The conception of reality	117
6.3.2.	The two kinds of conception of the 'self'	119
6.3.3.	The relationship between the cycle of awakening and mirativity	121
6.4.	The extension to mirative meaning as the first-person effect of Japanese evidential -*rasi-i*	122

CHAPTER 7

Conclusion

127

References	131
Data Sources	137
Index	139

Abbreviations

1	first person	HONT	honorific title
2	second person	HS	hearsay evidential
3	third person	IMM.PST	immediate past
ABL	ablative	IMP	imperative
ADD	additive	IMPF	imperfective aspect
ADN	adnominal	INF	infinitive
ADNZ	adnominalizer	INFR	inferential evidential
ADV	adverbal	INT	interrogative
ADVP	adverbial participle	LOC	locative
ADVRS	adversative	MIR	mirative
AFF	affirmative	NARR	narrative
ALL	allative	NEG	negative
APP	apparent	NMLZ	nominalizer
AS	adjectival suffix	NOM	nominative case
COMIT	comitative	NONFIRSTH	non-firsthand
COP	copula	NPST	non-past
COMPL	completive	OBJ	objective case
CONC	concessive	PERF	perfect
COND	conditional	POL	polite
CSL	causal	PST	past tense
DAT	dative case	PP	postpositional particle
DECL	declarative	PRES	present tense
DES	desiderative	PROCOMP	procomplement
DIST	distal	PROG	progressive aspect
DISTR	distributive	PROX	proximal
DQ	direct quotative	QUOT	quotative
EPI	epistemic modality	REP	reported evidential
EV	evidential	RES	resultative aspect
f, FEM	feminine	RST	restrictive
FIRSTH	firsthand	S	(intransitive) subject function
FN	formal noun	SEP	sentence ending particle
GEN	genitive case	SEQUENCE	sequence
GER	gerundive	SG	singular
HON	honorific	SUBJ	subjunctive

SUBR	subordinator
TOP, T.M	topic marker
TS	tense
VBLZ-PST	verbalization-past
VCLASS	verb class
VS	verbal suffix

List of Figures

Figure 2.1. The modality construction in Japanese ⋯⋯ 16
Figure 2.2. Blending in epistemic assessment ⋯⋯ 28
Figure 2.3. (Non-)parasitic expressions of mirativity ⋯⋯ 30
Figure 3.1. Conceptual substrate ⋯⋯ 35
Figure 3.2. Degree of subjectivity ⋯⋯ 36
Figure 3.3. Subjectification due to attenuation ⋯⋯ 38
Figure 3.4. Grounding ⋯⋯ 40
Figure 3.5. Clausal grounding ⋯⋯ 41
Figure 3.6. Reality model ⋯⋯ 42
Figure 3.7. Layering structure ⋯⋯ 43
Figure 3.8. The reversible figure 'Rubin's vase' ⋯⋯ 44
Figure 3.9. Embodied cognition ⋯⋯ 45
Figure 3.10. The mode of cognition ⋯⋯ 46
Figure 3.11. Information of knowledge and experience ⋯⋯ 48
Figure 3.12. The cycle of awakening ⋯⋯ 50
Figure 4.1. The extension of preposition *in* ⋯⋯ 66
Figure 4.2. The suffixal usage and the evidential usage (inference parameter) of *-rasi-i* ⋯⋯ 91
Figure 4.3. Hearsay parameter ⋯⋯ 93
Figure 5.1. Conceptual substrate (= Fig. 3.1) ⋯⋯ 99
Figure 5.2. The relationship between focalizer and focalized ⋯⋯ 101
Figure 5.3. The Japanese and English construal in type 1 ⋯⋯ 107
Figure 5.4. Japanese and English construal in type 2 ⋯⋯ 109
Figure 6.1. Reality model (= Fig. 3.6) ⋯⋯ 118
Figure 6.2. The mode of cognition (=Fig. 3.10) ⋯⋯ 119
Figure 6.3. The cycle of awakening (=Fig. 3.12) ⋯⋯ 122
Figure 6.4. The emergence of mirative meaning ⋯⋯ 124

List of Tables

Table 2.1. Verbal categories ⋯ 7
Table 2.2. Shifters and nonshifters ⋯ 7
Table 2.3. The parameters of evidentiality ⋯ 10
Table 2.4. Semantic parameters in evidential systems ⋯ 11
Table 2.5. Types of modality ⋯ 25
Table 2.6. Inferential evidentiality = Epistemic necessity ⋯ 26
Table 4.1. The model of extension (context-induced reinterpretation) ⋯ 65
Table 4.2. The process of producing function words ⋯ 70
Table 4.3. The two methods of function word development ⋯ 70
Table 4.4. The historical division of Japanese ⋯ 72
Table 4.5. The language change of the evidential marker - *gena* ⋯ 74
Table 4.6. The language change of - *soo=da* ⋯ 75
Table 4.7. The language change of evidentiality in Japanese ⋯ 76
Table 4.8. The language change of evidential - *rasi-i* ⋯ 81
Table 4.9. The data published from 1900 till 1950 ⋯ 85
Table 4.10. The data from novels published since 2000 ⋯ 85
Table 5.1. Genette (1972)'s three types of focalization ⋯ 99
Table 5.2. English expressions corresponding to the evidential - *rasi-i* in Japanese ⋯ 104
Table 5.3. Classification of the evidential - *rasi-i* and its correspondents in English ⋯ 104
Table 6.1. Examples of evidential - *rasi-i* in combination with a first-person pronoun ⋯ 122

CHAPTER 1

Introduction

The central claim of cognitive grammar (CG) is that linguistic phenomena are semantically and functionally motivated by human cognition. In other words, the purpose of studying linguistic phenomena from the perspective of CG is not merely to analyze language structure and meaning, but rather to recognize the human cognitive abilities that are reflected in our language when we use and understand a language. This approach assumes that meaning is a conceptualization adapted to linguistic conventions. The mental universe represented by language descriptions is not a world that exists independent of us. Most importantly our construal, that is how we conceptualize the world, is reflected in this mental universe. In this sense, the mental universe represented by linguistic expressions is a product constructed by cognitive activity based on our subjective views. It is different from the physical universe studied in physics. Therefore, the essential reason behind studying languages from the perspective of CG is to investigate how we create and share the mental universe depicted by language descriptions in our daily usage of language.

This book focuses on a nature of evidentiality, especially as expressed by the Japanese evidential *-rasi-i*. The linguistic category of evidentiality refers to the source of the information that serves as the basis for a proposition represented by an utterance. I will propose that a proper analysis of evidentiality is possible only if our conception of reality is understood as a cyclical process consisting of the repeated collapse and reconstruction of our mental universe caused by our embodied interactions. While absent in most Indo-European languages, evidential markers are found in minority languages such as American Indian languages (cf. Aikhenvald 2004). Various CG theories, including Langacker's (2008), have been constructed based on studies of English, which lacks any grammatical evidential markers and instead supplements meaning with lexical items if required. To analyze evidentiality from the perspective of CG, we must examine whether existing theoretical frameworks can be applied to the analysis of evidentiality. If not, then we need to improve them or replace them with a new approach. In this book, while primarily adhering to pre-existing CG frameworks in my analysis of evidentiality, I also introduce my own modifications and alternate frameworks where necessary by incorporating findings from philosophy and psychology (see Section 3.5).

I mainly focus on the Japanese evidential marker *-rasi-i* (hereinafter referred to as 'evidential *-rasi-i*'). There are two ways in which *-rasi-i* is used: its suffixal usage and its evidential usage. The suffixal usage of *-rasi-i*, as exemplified by (1a), signifies 'a typical image of a person, things, or events, which people generally have' (Teramura 1984: 243). The evidential marker *-rasi-i* can express two different evidential parameters: either inference or hearsay. The former, as exemplified by (1b), denotes the extrapolation of information through observation, while the latter, as exemplified by (1c), denotes extrapolation based on information conveyed to the speaker by others.[1]

(1) a. *Kare=wa totemo otoko-rasi-i.* [Typicality]
3SG=TOP very man-AS-NPST.
'He is very real man.'
b. *Tanaka=no heya=no dentoo=ga kie-te ir-u.*
Tanaka=GEN room=GEN light=NOM turn off-GER be-NPST
dooyara ne-te ir-u-rasi-i. [Inference]
apparently sleep-GER be-NPST-INFR-NPST
'Look at Tanaka's room The light is out, so he must be in bed.'
c. *tizin=no hanasi=de=wa, ano mise=no keieisya=ga*
acquaintance=GEN story=COP.INF=TOP DIST shop=GEN owner=NOM
kawat-ta-rasi-i. [Hearsay]
change-PST-HS-NPST
'My friend told me that the owner of the shop had changed.'
(Nihongo-Kijyutu-Bunpoo-Kenkyukai 2003: 168–169)

This book will attempt to answer the following three questions regarding evidentiality:

I. What motivates the grammaticalization of evidential *-rasi-i* from its suffixal usage?
II. What is the difference between evidentiality and epistemic modality?
III. Why does mirative meaning arise when evidential *-rasi-i* is combined with first-person pronouns?

This book is organized as follows. First, in Chapter 2, I summarize the basic understanding of evidentiality, referring mainly to Aikhenvald (2004). This chapter explains how evidentiality is divided into six categories semantically, and how the ways in which their meanings are encoded morpho-syntactically depend on the grammatical system of the particular languages in question. In addition, previous studies on evidentiality in Japanese linguistics are reviewed. After summarizing these basic understandings of evidentiality, I provide an overview of previous studies on the three issues stated above. In Chapter 3, I introduce several frameworks of cognitive linguistics relevant to the subject at hand, and propose my own framework for analyzing evidentiality from the framework of cognitive linguistics. In Chapter 4, I discuss in detail the issues surrounding the language change of evidential marker *-rasi-i*. The Japanese evidential marker *-rasi-i* is evidently a special case, having developing from an adjective-forming suffix, a course of language change different from that of evidentials in other languages. For this reason, it can serve as valuable data from the perspective of typology. In Chapter 5, I address the question of the difference between evidentiality and epistemic modality. Previous studies of the relationship between these two reached different conclusions, viewing them as either; i) the same category, ii) partially overlapping categories, or iii) completely different categories. From my perspective, evidentiality and epistemic modality are cognitive functions operating complementarily to arrive at a judgement about the reality of the situation described. In support of this understanding, I explore the differences between Japanese and English in the ways they prefer to express evidentiality, citing data taken from novels. Finally, in Chapter 6, I discuss the issue of mirativity as it relates to evidential *-rasi-i*. I consider the mirative extension of evidential *-rasi-i*, which implies an additional meaning of evidentiality in combination with first-person pronouns, and explore how and why the additional meaning is implied.

    By conceptualizing the environment around us, we construct our own mental universe, representing it by means of language expressions. The manner of conceptualization is constructed through our interactions with the environment because the cognitive ability to conceptualize our environment is reflected in language expressions. In other words, language is a tool to construe the world around us. From this perspective, language ability is not innate, but rather acquired through our general cognitive ability to construe the world. Previous studies on evidentiality have argued the definition of its meaning, namely whether the source of information behind the utterance is direct or indirect, or whether the information is based on perception, inference or hearsay. Other studies have described the relevant phenomena in their relationship with other grammatical elements or considered how evidential meanings are encoded morpho-syntactically. In contrast, this book is devoted to revealing how evidentiality reflects a cycle of collapse and reconstruction of our mental universe through our embodied interactions with the environment around us. By investigating Japanese evidentiality, I expect this book to contribute toward adding a fresh dimension to CG theory, which has until now been based primarily on studies of English.

Notes

1 Regarding the transcription of the Japanese into the Roman alphabet, Kunrei style of romanizations is adopted except for the name of persons, which are written in Hepburn romanization.

CHAPTER 2
Evidentiality

2.1. Introduction

The study of evidentiality can be traced to Boas (1938), who had studied Native American languages such as the Siouan language Lakota in the early 1900s. He pointed out that evidentiality had attracted less attention than it deserved because of the relative paucity of grammatical evidentiality markers in Indo-European languages. The concept received increased attention in the 2000s due to the work of Aikhenvald (2004), who studied linguistic phenomena related to evidentiality all over the world.

Aikhenvald (2004: 3) defines evidentiality as follows: 'Evidentiality is a linguistic category whose primary meaning is source of information.' Languages which have evidential markers are broadly divided into two types. The first type has obligatory evidentiality encoded in its grammar, while the other type has no uniform category for evidential meaning, which can instead be 'scattered' over its grammar (cf. Aikhenvald 2004: Ch.3). For example, Native American languages and many Eurasian languages possess an obligatory evidentiality system, whereas Romance and Germanic languages mark evidential meaning with lexical items.

First, in Sections 2.1 and 2.2, I summarize the basic understanding of evidentiality, referring mainly to Aikhenvald (2004). This chapter explains how evidentiality is divided into six semantic categories, and how the ways in which evidential meanings are encoded morpho-syntactically depend on the grammatical system of the particular languages in question. In Section 2.3, previous studies on evidentiality in Japanese are reviewed. In Sections 2.4 to 2.6, I provide an overview of previous studies on the three issues stated in Chapter 1. I will attempt to answer the following three questions regarding evidentiality:

I. What motivates the grammaticalization of evidential *-rasi-i* from the suffixal usage of *-rasi-i* ?

II. What is the difference between evidentiality and epistemic modality?
III. Why does mirative meaning arise when evidential *-rasi-i* is combined with first-person pronouns?

Regarding the first issue of the language change of evidential *-rasi-i*, Section 2.4 of my survey focuses on the work of Aikhenvald (2011), discussing the source of evidential markers worldwide and the kinds of grammatical paths through which they developed. The language change of the Japanese evidential marker *-rasi-i* is evidently a special case, having developed through yet a different path, namely from an adjective-forming suffix. For this reason, it can serve as valuable data from the perspective of typology. I address the second issue above in Section 2.5, where I provide an overview of the three main positions on the relationship between evidentiality and epistemic modality, namely that they are to be viewed as: i) the same category, ii) partially overlapping categories, or iii) completely different categories. After surveying previous studies, I reach the conclusion that evidentiality and epistemic modality are cognitive functions operating complementarily to arrive at a judgement about the reality of the situation described. In Section 2.6, after reviewing the definition of mirativity and the first-person effect, I consider the mirative extension of evidential *-rasi-i*, which implies an additional meaning of evidentiality in combination with first-person pronouns. Although many previous studies have defined mirativity either morpho-syntactically or semantically, it is reasonable to suppose that mirativity is a cognitive phenomenon of the awakening that takes place in the course of renewing ordinary knowledge. Finally, in Section 2.7, I summarize this chapter and restate the three issues in detail.

2.2. The parameters of evidentiality and how they are marked

Jakobson (1990) was the first to formulate evidentiality as a grammatical item. He cast a spotlight on the deictic nature of grammatical items and described grammatical categories using two criteria, as described below:

(1) 1. Speech itself (^{s}), and its topic, the narrated matter (^{n});
    2. [T]he event itself (E), and any of its participants (P), whether "performer" or "undergoer"

(Jakobson 1990: 390)

In his theory, there are two binary options. One is the dichotomy between 'speech itself' and 'the narrated matter,' the other that between 'the event itself' and 'participants.' Consequently, four items are to be distinguished: a narrated event (E^n), a speech event (E^s), a participant of a narrated event (P^n), and a participant of a speech event (P^s) (Jakobson 1990: 390). He characterized the grammatical category PERSON [P^n/P^s] as the person who is a participant of the narrated event with reference to the participants of the speech event (i.e. the speaker, the hearer, or the third person). TENSE [E^n/E^s] was characterized as the narrated event with reference to the speech event. The others were summarized as below:

Table 2.1. Verbal categories

Reference to narrated item	Participant involved		Participant not involved	
	Designator	Connector	Designator	Connector
Nonshifter	Qualifier: Gender	Voice	Qualifier: Status	Taxis
	Quantifier: Number		Quantifier: Aspect	
Shifter	Person	Mood	Tense	Evidential

(Jakobson 1990: 391)

Table 2.2. Shifters and nonshifters

Reference to narrated item	Participant involved		Participant not involved	
	Designator	Connector	Designator	Connector
Nonshifter	P^n	$P^n E^n$	E^n	$E^n E^n$
Shifter	P^n/P^s	$P^n E^n/P^s$	E^n/E^s	$E^n E^{ns}/E^s$

(Jakobson 1990: 391)

Evidentiality was formulated in his theory as follows:

(2) $E^n E^{ns}/E^s$) EVIDENTIAL is a tentative label for this verbal category which takes into account three events — a narrated event, a speech event, and a narrated speech event (E^{ns}). The speaker reports an event on the basis of someone else's report (quotative, i.e. hearsay evidence), of a dream (relative evidence), of a guess (presumptive evidence), or of his own previous experience (memory evidence).

(Jakobson 1990: 392)

Jakobson (1990) stated that evidentiality consists of three kinds of events: a narrated event E^n, a speech event E^s, or a narrated speech event E^{ns}. The last, E^{ns}, is an event that alleges the source of information regarding the narrated event (e.g. someone else's report or presumptive evidence). An evidentiality has two semantically oppositional terms related to E^{ns} and E^s: 'direct narration' ($E^{ns} = E^s$) and 'indirect narration' ($E^{ns} \neq E^s$). Given that he presented evidentiality as 'a tentative label' and included in his definition E^{ns}, which he did not use to formulate any other categories, Jakobson (1990) intended to define a category different from other grammatical categories such as TENSE or MOOD.

Delancey (1997) divided evidentiality into three sub-categories. His category 'direct visual knowledge' corresponded to Jakobson's (1990) 'direct narration.' The 'indirect narration' category proposed by Jakobson (1990) was divided into two categories: 'inferential,' which expresses 'a conclusion reached from evidence,' and 'hearsay,' which refers to the reporting of information obtained from someone else.

(3) This system illustrates several common evidential categories: direct visual knowledge, typically the unmarked member of the system; inferential, indicating that the content of the statement is a conclusion reached from evidence rather direct perception, and hearsay, reporting information which the speaker obtained from someone else.

(DeLancey 1997: 35)

From the perspective of cross-linguistic studies, Aikhenvald (2004) stated that evidential meaning the world over can be categorized into six semantic parameters based on the source of information.

(4) The semantic parameters of evidentials
    I.   VISUAL: covers information acquired through seeing.
    II. NON-VISUAL: covers information acquired through hearing, and is typically extended to smell and taste, and sometimes also to touch.
    III. INFERENCE: based on visible or tangible evidence, or result.
    IV. ASSUMPTION: based on evidence other than visible results: this may include logical reasoning, assumption, or simply general knowledge.
    V. HEARSAY: for reported information with no reference to those it was reported by.
    VI. QUOTATIVE: for reported information with an overt reference to the quoted source.

(Aikhenvald 2004: 64)

Aikhenvald (2004) subdivided each of the three categories proposed by DeLancey (1997) to produce these six parameters. The 'sensory parameters' corresponding to the 'direct narration' of Jakobsen (1990) and Delancey (1997) is further subdivided into two subcategories of obtaining information through direct experience: (I) visual and (II) non-visual. For example, the Papuan language Oksapmin has a non-visual marker. If the information has been obtained visually, the verb is unmarked as in (5). If, on the other hand, an event has been perceived through something other than one's visual sense, such as in (6), it is expressed 'by using a verb stem (with a sequential marker) plus the verb "do".' (Aikhenvald 2004: 47).

Oksapmin

(5) yot   haan   ihitsi   nuhur   waaihpaa
    two   men   they:two   we   went:down
    'Two other men and I went down' (I saw it)

(Aikhenvald 2004: 46)

(6) barus apri-s   ha-h
    Plane come-SEQUENCE   do-IMM.PST
    'I hear the plane coming'

(Aikhenvald 2004: 47)

The 'inference parameters,' which include (III) inference and (IV) assumption, correspond to DeLancey's (1997) 'inference' category. In Tsafiki, a language spoken in Ecuador, which has both inference and assumption markers, the evidential marker -*nu* is employed if the information has been obtained through inference from direct physical evidence as in (7). If, on the other hand, the information is assumed based on general knowledge, a nominalization followed by the verb class marker -*n-ki* is used, as shown in (8).

Tsafiki

(7) Manuel   ano   fi-*nu*-e
    Manuel   food   eat-INFR=DECL
    'Manuel ate' (the speaker sees the dirty dishes)

(Aikhenvald 2004: 54)

(8) Manuel   ano   fi-*n-ki*-e
    Manuel   food   eat-NOML-VCLASS: do-DECL
    'Manuel ate' (he always eats at eight o'clock and it's now nine o'clock)

(Aikhenvald 2004: 54)

The 'reported parameters,' which include (V) hearsay and (VI) quotative, are equivalent to the 'hearsay' category proposed by DeLancey (1997). The Uto-Aztecan language Cora has both hearsay and quotative markers. Information obtained from a secondhand report is marked with the particle *nú'u*, as shown in (9), while information quoted from a story is marked with the particle *yée* in (10).

Cora
(9) *Ayáa pá **nú'u** tyú-hu'-u-ri h*
 thus SUBJ QUOT DISTR-NARR-COMPL-do
 'This is, they say, what took place.'

(Aikhenvald 2004: 57)

(10) *Y-én peh **yée** wa-híhwa mʷáa,*
 here-TOP 2.SUBR QUOT COMPL-yell 2SG
 Yáa pú nú'u hí tʲí-r-aa-ta-hée
 PROCOMP SUBJ REP DISTR-DISTR:SG-COMPL-PERF-tell
 '"From right up on top here, you will call out loud and clear", that is what she called on him to do.'

(Aikhenvald 2004: 57, glosses are mine)

Previous studies on evidentiality are summarized below. In my discussion of Japanese evidentiality in this book, I adopt the DeLancey's terminology.

Table 2.3. The parameters of evidentiality

Jakobson (1990)	Direct narration		Indirect narration			
DeLancey (1997)	Sensory		Inference		Reported	
Aikhenvald (2004)	Visual	Non-visual	Inference	Assumption	Hearsay	Quotative

Evidentials are expressed in a variety of ways. The parameters listed in Table 2.3 are expressed differently in different languages. With respect to how evidentiality is marked, there are four kinds of languages worldwide.

(11) Ways of marking evidentiality
 When it comes to marking evidentiality, there are four basic types of languages:
 a. Languages that have a grammatical evidential system. These languages have obligatory evidentiality markers.
 b. Languages that have grammatical evidential markers, but do not have to mention them in every sentence.
 c. Languages that have no grammatical evidential markers. These languages supplement the meaning of evidentiality with lexical items.
 d. Languages that have 'evidential strategies,' in which categories and

forms acquire secondary meanings related to evidentiality.

The languages that belong to the (11a) category have a grammatical evidential system in which evidential markers are obligatory. Aikhenvald (2004: Ch.2) further subdivided these languages as follows.[1] The semantic parameters of evidentiality are operational in different types of grammatical systems. Aikhenvald established five types of systems that possess 2 evidential choices (Type-A), five types that possess 3 choices (Type-B), three types that possess 4 choices (Type-C), and one type that possesses 5 choices (Type-D).

Table 2.4. Semantic parameters in evidential systems

Type-A Two choices	A1. Firsthand versus Non-firsthand
	A2. Non-firsthand versus 'everything else'
	A3. Reported (or hearsay) versus 'everything else'
	A4. Sensory evidence versus Reported (or hearsay)
	A5. Auditory (acquired through hearing) versus 'everything else'
Type-B Three choices	B1. Direct (or Visual), Inferred, Reported
	B2. Visual, Non-visual sensory, Inferred
	B3. Visual, Non-visual sensory, Reported
	B4. Non-visual Sensory, Inferred, Reported
	B5. Reported, Quotative, 'everything else'
Type-C Four choices	C1. Visual, Non-Visual Sensory, Inferred, Reported
	C2. Direct (or Visual), Inferred, Assumed, Reported
	C3. Direct, Inferred, Reported, Quotative
Type-D Five choices	D1. Visual, Non-Visual Sensory, Inferred, Assumed, Reported

The languages categorized in (11b) do not form an evidential system such as those mentioned in Table 2.4, but express evidential meanings in terms of certain grammatical markers. Referring to the Japanese evidential markers *-rasi-i*, *-yoo=da*, and *-soo=da*, Aikhenvald (2004: 81) suggested two possibilities regarding their typological position based on Aoki's (1986) work on Japanese evidentials. The first possibility is that Japanese is a Type-A3 system. The characteristics of a Type-A system are as follows:

(12) Type A: Two-term system
    A1. Firsthand versus Non-firsthand;
    A2. Non-firsthand versus 'everything else';

A3. Reported (or 'hearsay') versus 'everything else';
A4. Sensory Evidence versus Reported (or 'hearsay');
A5. Auditory (acquired through hearing) versus 'everything else'

(Aikhenvald 2004: 25)

This would mean that Japanese has a binary evidential system: reported information is marked overtly, but no markers is used to denote everything else, which describes events based on unspecified information and is known as an evidentially neutral form. The other possibility is that Japanese does not possess a rigorous evidential system for obligatorily marking the source of information, but instead has evidential markers that are optional. The unclear nature of the Japanese evidential system is demonstrated by following examples:

(13) a. *Taro=no   hanasi=de=wa,   ano   mise=no oonaa=ga   kawat-ta*
       Taro=GEN telling=COP.INF=TOP DIST shop=GEN owner=NOM,   change-PST
       {-soo=da / -rasi-i}.   [Hearsay]
       {-HS=COP / -HS-NPST}.
       'Taro told me that the shop's owner had changed.'
    b. *Kaisoo   go=no   mise=o   mir-u=to,   ano   mise=no*
       renovation after=GEN shop=OBJ see-NPST=COND, DIST shop=GEN
       oonaa=wa   kawat-ta   {-soo=da / -rasi-i}.*   [inference]
       owner=NOM change-PST {*-HS=COP / -INFR-NPST}
       'Seeing the renovated shop, (I could tell that) the shop's owner had changed.'

As pointed out by Aikhenvald (2004), '[finite clause] *-so=da*' is a dedicated marker that indicates hearsay, which is information that has been obtained from someone else. Therefore, it is appropriate to classify the marker as one that fits into the A3 system. However, '[finite clause] *-rasi-i*' is a marker used for denoting information that is obtained indirectly, such as an inference from evidence or hearsay. Accordingly, this marker fits into the A2 system (non-firsthand versus everything else). Thus, Japanese possesses two types of evidential marker. This lends support to the view that Japanese does not possess a rigid evidential system, but instead utilizes optional grammatical items to express evidentiality.

The languages grouped under (11c) do not have any grammatical markers that denote evidentiality, but instead supplement evidential meaning with lexical items. Examples include English, in which adverbials and verb phrases are used for indicating evidential meaning, as shown in (14). Whether a given optional marker indicating evidentiality is a grammatical one or a lexical one depends on the grammatical system possessed by the language in question. The terms *allegedly* and *seem* in (14) represent a reported parameter and an inference parameter, respectively. They have the grammatical character of adverbial and verb phrases in English, and thus the status of lexical items.

(14) a. The author is *allegedly* a member of a comedy troupe and presumably was trying to be witty.
 b. It *seems* to be a good movie.

(Cornillie 2009: 46)

The languages in (11d) indicate evidentiality by using evidentiality strategies, in which non-evidential categories acquire semantic extensions that enable them to convey the source of information.

(15) Evidentiality strategies: use of a non-evidential category (such as tense, aspect, or modality) to refer to an information source.

(Aikhenvald 2004: 392)

It has been pointed out that the perfect tense is closely related to indirect evidentials cross-linguistically. It is not completely unrelated to indirect evidentials that denote inferences from present evidence since it denotes 'current relevance.' In other words, an event from the past can be related to the present by producing results or leaving traces of something in the past. Although the grammatical evidential markers in a language are used to express the source of information, the markers used as evidentiality strategies do not have any one particular meaning. Rather, one of their functions is that of expressing evidential meaning. For example, the perfect form in Gerogian also possesses non-firsthand evidential meaning related to a statement's source of information.

(16) *varsken-s   ianvr-is   rva-s   p'irvel-ad   (φ-) u-c'am-eb-i-a*
 Varsken-DAT January-GEN 9-DAT first-ADV (he-) ov-torture-TS-PREF-her
 šušanik'-i.
 Shushanik'-NOM
 'Varsken apparently first tortured Shushanik on 8th January.'

(Aikhenvald 2004: 113)

In Georgian, the perfect form is also employed to express the present perfect tense, as in English (e.g. *How many deer have I and your grandfather killed?*), and 'it can be used to refer to present, to future, or as a kind of imperative or optative. That is, the Georgian system is adequately interpreted as an evidentiality strategy rather than evidentiality proper' (Aikhenvald 2004: 113).

2.3. Evidentiality in Japanese

In this section, I overview previous studies related to Japanese evidentiality. Aoki's (1986) pioneering research on Japanese evidentiality outlined the following items as evidential markers:

(17) I. Indirect evidential *-garu*
   A marker expressing that a given feeling or experience belongs not to the speaker, but to another.
   II. *-no, -n*
   A marker expressing the speaker's confidence in the veracity of information that is ordinarily directly unknowable.
   III. Modals of indirect evidential *-rasi-i, -soo=da*
   Markers expressing that the speaker is cognizant of the information, whether through 'hearsay' or 'inference.'

In Japanese, sensory adjectives such as *samu-i* 'cold' and *kanasi-i* 'sad' can only be used to describe the internal state of speaker, but not that of another. In the latter case, the indirect evidential *-garu* must be used, to express the fact that the speaker is basing the statement on inferences gleaned from the other's appearance.

(18) **Kare=wa*   *atu-i.*
     3SG=TOP   hot-NPST
     'He is hot.'
     **Kare=wa*   *samu-i.*
     3SG=TOP   cold-NPST
     'He is cold'
     **Kare=wa*   *sabisi-i.*
     3SG=TOP   lonely-NPST
     'He is lonely'

(Aoki 1986: 224, glosses are mine)

(19) *Kare=wa*   *atu-gat-te*   *ir-u.*
     3SG=TOP   hot-EV-GER   be-NPST
     'He is hot.'
     **Kare=wa*   *samu-gat-te*   *ir-u.*
     3SG=TOP   cold-EV-GER be-NPST

'He is cold'
*Kare=wa   sabisi-gat-te ir-u.
3SG=TOP   lonely-EV-GER be-NPST
'He is lonely'

(Aoki 1986: 224–225, glosses are mine)

By the same token, the marker -no/-n can also be used to describe another's internal state. Aoki (1986: 228) recognized the evidential markers as follows: 'An evidential no, or more informal n, may be used to state that the speaker is convinced that for some reason what is ordinarily directly unknowable is nevertheless true.'

(20) *Kare=wa   atu-i=no=da.*
    3SG=TOP hot=NMLZ=COP
    'I know that he is hot. It is a fact that he is hot.'

(Aoki 1986: 229, glosses are mine)

The third type of evidential marker in Japanese outlined by traditional Japanese studies is evidential modality. *Nihongo-Kijjyutu-Bunpou-Kenkyukai* (2003, hereinafter NKBK) defined evidentiality as 'categories of forms describing recognition based on some evidence,' citing *-rasi-i*, *-soo=da*, *-yoo=da* and *-mitai=da* as examples of evidential modality.[2] These evidential modalities denote inference based on speaker-observed evidence and hearsay. In other words, they represent information presented by the speaker that they obtained from others.

(21) INFERENCE
    a. *Sakuya   ame=ga   hut-ta   { -yoo=da / -mitai=da / -rasi-i}.*
       last night rain-NOM fall-PST {-INFR=COP / -INFR=COP / -INFR-NPST}
       'It seems that it rained last night.'
    b. *Kono   keeki=wa   oisi-soo=da.*
       PROX cake=TOP delicious-INFR=COP
       'This cake seems delicious.'

(22) HEARSAY
    Sensei=no   hanasi=ni   yoru=to,   Suzuki=wa   ryuugaku-suru
    teacher=GEN story=DAT accord=COND, Suzuki=TOP education abroad-VS
    {-soo=da / -rasi-i}.
    {-HS=COP / -HS-NPST}
    'According to my teacher, Mr. Suzuki is going to study abroad.'

When appended to a word base, the evidential markers -*yoo=da*, -*mitai=da* and -*soo=da* serve as inference markers, as is demonstrated by the sentences in (21). When appended to a finite clause, -*rasi-i* and -*soo=da* function as hearsay markers, as can be observed in (22). Although they are not required when describing information related to the speaker, these indirect evidentials are needed when speakers describe information that they cannot access directly, such as another's internal state.

The evidential modalities examined in this book possess a layering structure in which they encompass a proposition, as illustrated below.

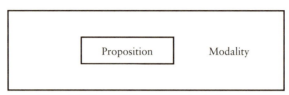

Figure 2.1. The modality construction in Japanese

Evidential modalities are appended to the non-past/past form of verbs and adjectives (NKBK 2003), as exemplified by (23).

(23) a. *Tanaka-san=wa* {*kur-u* / *ki-ta*}   {-*rasi-i* /-*yoo=da* /-*mitai=da* /-*soo=da*}. [Verb]
  Mr. Tanaka=TOP {come-NPST /come.PST} {-EV-NPST / -EV=COP / -EV=COP / -HS=COP}
  'It seems / I hear that Mr. Tanaka will come / came.'
 b. *Kono meron=wa* {*taka-i* / *taka-kat-ta*}   { -*rasi-i* / -*yoo=da* /
  PROX melon=TOP {expensive-NPST / expensive-VBLZ-PST} {-EV-NPST/-EV=COP
  /-*mitai=da* / -*soo=da*}.   [adjective]
  / -EV=COP /-HS=COP}
  'It seems / I hear that this melon is/was expensive.'

The conjugation differs when they are appended to noun or nominal adjectives, and there are differences in the form to which the different evidential markers attach, as seen in (24), (25), and (26). The evidential -*rasi-i* and -*mitai=da* are both appended to the word base of nouns and nominal adjectives, while -*yoo=-da* is appended to the adverbial form of nominal adjectives and the construction noun + -*no*. The evidential -*soo=da* is appended to any finite form.

(24) a. *Ano atari=wa*   {*sizuka* / *sizuka=dat-ta*} {-*rasi-i* / -*mitai=da*}. [Nominal adjective]
   DIST place=TOP {quiet / quiet=COP-PST} {-EV-NPST /-EV=COP}
   'It seems / I heard that it is/was quiet around there.'
  b. *Tokyo=wa*   {*ame* / *ame=dat-ta*}   {-*rasi-i* / -*mitai=da*}.   [Noun]
   Tokyo=TOP {rain / rain=COP-PST} {-EV-PST/ -EV=COP}

'It seems / I heard that it rains/rained in Tokyo.'

(25) a. *Ano atari=wa {sizuka=na / sizuka=dat-ta} -yoo=da.* [Nominal adjective]
   DIST place=TOP {quiet=COP.ADN/ quiet=COP-PST} -INFER=COP
   'It seems that it is/was quiet around there.'
   b. *Tokyo=wa {ame=no / ame=dat-ta} -yoo=da.* [Noun]
   Tokyo-TOP {rain=ADNZ/ rain=COP-PST}-INFR=COP
   'It seems that it rains/rained in Tokyo.'

(26) a. *Ano atari=wa {sizuka=da / sizuka=dat-ta} -soo=da.* [Nominal adjective]
   DIST place=TOP {quiet=COP /quiet=COP-PST} - HS=COP
   'I heard that it is/was quiet around there.'
   b. *Tokyo=wa {ame=da / ame=dat-ta} -soo=da.* [Noun]
   Tokyo=TOP {rain=COP /rain=COP-PST} -HS=COP
   'I heard that it rains/rained in Tokyo.'

Every evidential marker follows a finite clause. Thus, Japanese evidential modalities comprise a layered construction wherein they embrace the proposition.³

Japanese modalities are subcategorized into epistemic modalities and evidential modalities, which differ in their patterns of reasoning. There are three patterns of reasoning, which are described below.

(27) The three types of reasoning
   Deduction: the inference of particular instances by referring to a general law or principle.
   - Modus ponens
Premise 1:	All men are mortal.	(P → Q)
Premise 2:	Socrates is a man.	(P)
Conclusion:	Therefore, Socrates is mortal.	(Q)
   - Modus tollens
Premise 1:	All men are mortal.	(P → Q)
Premise 2:	X is not mortal.	(¬ Q)
Conclusion:	Therefore, X is not a man.	(¬ P)

   Induction: the inference of a general law from particular instances.
Premise 1:	Suzuki from the Tohoku region is kind.	(P ∧ R→Q)
Premise 2:	Tanaka from the Tohoku region is kind.	(P ∧ S→Q)
Conclusion:	People from the Tohoku region are kind.	(P→Q)

   Abduction: the inference of the cause through the observation of a phenomenon.
Premise 1:	If it rains, the ground gets wet.	(P → Q)
Premise 2:	The ground has gotten wet.	(Q)

Conclusion: It rained. (P)

Deduction typically involves syllogism, which is the process of reaching a conclusion by thinking about facts that are assumed to be true. Induction seeks to generalize and abstract the commonality (P) from given instances. It is deeply related to general human cognitive activities, much like categorization. There is no assurance that abductive reasoning will always result in a reasonable inference, but it is a necessary form of reasoning in everyday human life because it facilitates the inference of causation through the observation of a phenomenon (cf. Yonemori 2007).

Kinoshita (1998, 2009) proposed that Japanese modalities could be subcategorized into epistemic modalities (e.g. -kamosirena-i, -nitigaina-i, -hazu=da) and evidential modalities (e.g. -yoo=da, -rasi-i), each of which follow different patterns of reasoning.[4]

(28) Premise 1: If a house is old, there is a mouse in the house. (P → Q)

(29) Premise 2: The speaker knows that the house is old. (P)
    a. *(dooyara) Ano ie=ni=wa nezumi=ga
    (perhaps) DIST house=LOC=TOP mouse=NOM
    ir-u {-yoo=da / -rasi-i}. (Q)
    be-NPST {-INFR=COP /-INFR-NPST}
    '(Perhaps) There is a mouse in that house.'
    b. Ano ie=ni=wa nezumi=ga ir-u {-kamosirena-i /-nitigaina-i /-hazu=da}. (Q)
    DIST house=LOC=TOP mouse=NOM be-NPST {-EPI-NPST /-EPI-NPST /-EPI=COP}
    'There {may / must} be a mouse in that house.'

(30) Premise 2: The speaker knows that there is a mouse in the house. (Q)
    a. (dooyara) Ano ie=wa huru-i {-yoo=da / -rasi-i}. (P)
    (perhaps) DIST house=TOP old-NPST {-INFR=COP/ -INFR-NPST}
    'Perhaps that house is old.'
    b. Ano ie=wa huru-i {-kamosirena-i /-nitigaina-i /-hazu=da}. (P)
    DIST house=TOP old-NPST {-EPI-NPST /-EPI-NPST /-EPI-NPST}
    'That house {may / must} be old.'

Inference pattern (29) is based on the modus ponens of deduction, where the conclusion *There is a mouse in the house* is inferred from Premise 2 *The house is old* based on Premise 1 *If a house is old, there is a mouse in the house*. In this case, epistemic modalities can be used, but not evidential modalities. Inference pattern (30) utilizes abductive reasoning, wherein the cause *The house is old* is inferred from the conclusion *There is a mouse in the house* based on the premise *If a house is old, there is a mouse in the house*. In this situation, either epistemic modalities or evidential modalities can be used. Considering these facts, the inference pattern of evidential modalities must be the abductive one, where an unknown cause is inferred from a known conclusion.

Hearsay is when the speaker conveys information obtained from others. It requires three components: 1) a source of information, 2) a narrator (speaker), and 3) a listener. When the speaker conveys something to the listener, the sentence bearing the evidential marker uttered by the speaker implies the existence of a third party who conveyed the information to the speaker, as exemplified by the following:[5]

(31) A: *Eki   mae=ni   atarasi-i   kafe=ga   dekiru=yo.*
      Station   front-LOC new-NPST café=NOM open=SEP
      'A new café will open outside the station.'
   B: *Soo-rasi-i=ne.*
      so-HS-NPST=SEP
      'Apparently.'

Both hearsay and quotation have in common the function of conveying information to the listener that was acquired by the speaker from a third party. In quotation, indirect speech, and hearsay, the following deictic elements differ in certain respects from the utterance of the original speaker. The utterance in (33a) is reframed by the speaker into sentence (33b).

(32) a. demonstratives: e.g. *kore* (this), *are / sore* (that)
    b. words related to time: e.g. *kyoo* (today), *asita* (tomorrow)
    c. personal pronouns: e.g. *watasi* (I), *anata* (you)
    d. verbs related to deixis e.g. *iku* (go), *kuru* (come), *ageru* (give), *morau* (take)
    e. honorific words, sentence ending particles

(33) a. *Watasi=wa   asita   asoko=e   ik-u.*
      1SG=TOP   tomorrow DIST=ALL go-NPST
      'I will go there tomorrow.'
   b. *Ano   hito=wa   kyoo   koko-e   kur-u   {-soo=da /*
      DIST   person=TOP today DIST-ALL come-NPST {-HS=COP /
      to   it-te   ir-u}.
      QUOT say-GER be-NPST}
      'He/she is going to come here today.'

Nakahata (1992) also pointed out the following differences between hearsay and quotation:

(34)
  I. The original speaker can be specified in the sentence with a quotation marker, but does not have to be specified in the sentence with a hearsay marker.
  II. The quotation marker co-occurs with constructions expressing illocutionary force such as orders, questions, offers, and requests, whereas hearsay evidentials do not.
  III. The quotation marker has a past form (*-ta*) like *-to-it-ta* 'someone said that ... ,' while the hearsay evidential *-soo=da* does not possess a past form. The evidential *-rasi-i* is sometimes used in its past form as a hearsay evidential.
  IV. A sentence with a quotation marker represents the original speaker's mental attitude, but in a sentence with a hearsay marker, the original speaker's attitude is reframed from the perspective of the speaker that is conveying the information.

    e.g.) a. *Tanaka-san=wa*   '*watasi=ga*   *waru-kat-ta*'   *to it-te ir-u.*
            Mr. Tanaka=TOP   1SG=NOM   sorry-VBLZ-PST QUOT say-GER be-NPST
            'Mr. Tanaka said, "I'm sorry."'

      b. ? *Tanaka-san=wa (zibun=ga)*   *waru-kat-ta-soo=desu.*
         Mr. Tanaka=TOP   (1SG=NOM)   sorry-VBLZ-PST-HS=COP.HON
         'I heard from Mr. Tanaka that he's sorry.'

Sentence IV (b) is unacceptable because Japanese hearsay markers cannot convey the original speaker's mental attitude. Hearsay markers can only be used in statements that do not express the attitude of the original speaker.

(35) a. *Tanaka-san=wa suugaku=no*   *ten=ga*   *waru-kat-ta to it-te ir-u.*
     Mr. Tanaka=TOP   math=GEN   score=NOM   bad-VBLZ-PST QUOT say-GER be-NPST
     'Mr. Tanaka said "I had got bad marks in a math examination."'

    b. *Tanaka-san=wa suugaku=no*   *ten=ga*   *waru-kat-ta-soo=desu.*
     Mr. Tanaka=TOP   math=GEN   score=NOM   bad-VBLZ-PST-HS=COP.HON
     'I heard from Mr. Tanaka that he had got bad marks in a math examination.'

(Nakahata 1992: 20)

2.4. Where do evidentialities come from?

Aikhenvald (2011) showed that there are two main types of grammaticalization of evidentiality worldwide. One is traditional grammaticalization, in which a lexical item becomes a function word. The other is evidentiality strategy, which involves the use of a non-evidential category (such as tense, aspect, or modality) to refer to an information source.

(36) Grammaticalization of evidentials follows two general paths. Markers of evidentiality may develop out of grammaticalizing a lexical item: a verb, or, less frequently, a noun becomes a grammatical marker of information source within a closed system of choices. Alternatively, an evidential may evolve out of an evidentiality strategy, acquiring the status of a grammatical system in its own right.

(Aikhenvald 2011: 606)

In the first case, the following grammaticalization paths have been found:

(37) From a lexical item to a grammatical evidential
    a. From a verb to an evidential
       (a) Verbs of speech > markers of reported or quotative evidentials
          e.g.) Tsafiki: verb *ti-* 'say' > reported evidential *-ti-*
       (b) Verbs of perception > markers of visual or non-visual sensory evidentiality
          e.g.) Tariana: first-person singular of the verb *-ka* 'see' > visual evidential
          verb *-hima* 'hear, feel' > non-visual evidential *-mha*
       (c) Verbs of other semantic groups > various evidentials
          e.g.) Hupda: verb 'produce sound' > non-visual evidential (Hupda)
          East Tucanoan languages: verbs 'seem, be perceived, feel' > non-visual evidentials
          Wintu and Hupda: verbs referring to location or existence > inferred and assumed evidentials
    b. From a deictic or a locative to an evidential
       (a) deictic elements, locative or directional markers > evidentials
          e.g.) Wintu: proximal demonstrative 'this' > assumed evidential
          Sissala and Gur (Voltaic): locative demonstrative 'here, this' > hearsay or reported evidentials
    c. Nouns, or other word classes, as sources for evidentials
       (a) Noun
          e.g.) Xamatauteri and Yanomami: noun 'noise' > reported evidential
          Piro: noun 'sounds' > reported evidential
          Northern Samoyedic languages: noun 'voice' > non-visual

sensory evidential
Basque: noun *omen* 'rumor, fame, reputation' > reported particle
   (b) Adverbials
      e.g.) Wintu: adverbial morpheme 'maybe, potentially' > reported evidential
      West Greenlandic: adverbial morpheme 'probably' > inferential evidential

The second type of grammaticalization, which involves evidentiality strategies, includes the following.

(38) Evidentiality strategies as sources for evidentials
   a. Non-indicative modalities
      e.g.) French: Nonindicative modalities > non-first-hand evidentials
      Algonquian languages: Conjunct dubitative forms > non-first-hand evidentials
      Abkhaz and Circassian: Future marker > non-first-hand evidentials
      Hill Patwin: Auxiliary verb 'be (locational)' followed by the definite future suffix.
   b. Declarative and indicative modalities
      e.g.) Shipibo-Konibo: declarative-indicative marker > direct evidential
      Tariana: declarative marker > recent past visual evidential
   c. Perfect, resultative, past tense
      e.g.) Turkic, Iranian languages: anterior and perfect forms > non-first-hand evidential
      Cree, Montagnais, Naskapi: Proto-Algonquian perfect > non-first-hand evidential
      Dargwa and Archi: Complex resultative construction (perfective converbs and a copula) > non-first-hand evidentials
   d. Participles and other deverbal nominalizations
      e.g.) Nenets: nominalization > non-first-hand evidential (auditive)
      Komi: past particle > non-first-hand evidential
      Lithuanian: active participle > reported evidential
   e. Speech complements
      e.g.) Standard Estonian: the main verb of speech or perception and active participle > reported evidentials
   f. Copula constructions
      e.g.) Patwin: locational 'be' > direct sensory evidential
      Akha: copulas > non sensorial evidentials
      West Greenlandic: verbalizing affix and 3rd person singular indicative inflection 'it is so that' > reported evidential

Although Aikhenvald (2011) covered a wide range of grammaticalizations in various languages, evidential modalities in Japanese take a grammatical path different to any of them, having been grammaticalized from suffix-forming adjectives or adjectival verbs. This language change runs counter to the traditional grammaticalization pattern, which conforms to what is known as the 'unidirectional hypothesis' (cf. Hopper and Traugott 2003). Given this fact, revealing the process of the language change of evidential modalities in Japanese has significant value for cross-linguistic studies. I will discuss this and explore the rationale behind this process from the perspective of cognitive linguistics in Chapter 4.

2.5. Epistemic modality vs. evidentiality

The relationship between evidentiality and epistemic modality has often been discussed. According to De Haan (2010), there are four positions on the relationship between the two, which I will detail in this section.[6]

(39) **Positions on epistemic modality and evidentiality**
   a. Evidentiality is part of epistemic modality.
      (Palmer 1986)
   b. Evidentiality and epistemic modality are part of a larger domain.
      (Palmer 2001, the larger domain is called *propositional modality*)
   c. Evidentiality and epistemic modality partially overlap.
      (Van der Auwera and Plungian 1998, the area of overlap is inferentiality)
   d. Evidentiality and epistemic modality are separate domains.
      (De Haan 1999, Aikhenvald 2004)

(De Haan 2010: 106)

2.5.1. Palmer (1986)

Palmer (1986) considered evidentiality to be a form of epistemic modality that refers to the proposition as non-real. Palmer applied the term 'epistemic' not only to 'modal systems that basically involve the notions of possibility and necessity' but also to 'any modal system that indicates the degree of commitment by the speaker to what he says' (Palmer 1986: 51). In that sense, evidentiality constitutes a subcategory of epistemic modality. In particular, the epistemic modality presented by Palmer (1986) functions as a means of indicating that the speaker is not presenting what they are saying as fact. This indication occurs in one of the four forms mentioned below, of which (iii) is considered to be a reported parameter and (iv) to be an inference parameter.

(40) (i) that he is speculating about it
e.g.) It is possible that ... / I think that ...
(ii) that he is presenting it as a deduction
e.g.) It is to be concluded that ... / I conclude that ...
(iii) that he has been told about it
e.g.) It is said that ... / X said that ...
(iv) that it is a matter only of appearance, based on the evidence of (possibly fallible) senses.
e.g.) It appears that ...

Palmer (1986: 70) stated that '[i]t would be a futile exercise to try to decide whether a particular system (or even a term in a system in some cases) is evidential rather than a judgment,' which indicates that he opted not to distinguish the two categories.

The definition of epistemic modality proposed by Palmer (1986, 2001) as any way in which the speaker avoids presenting what they are saying as fact is wider than the usual definition. Based on the subcategories of epistemic modality he presents, it can be argued that their process of reasoning can be distinguished in some fashion. Thus, there should be some difference between evidentiality and epistemic modality.

2.5.2. Van der Auwera and Plugian (1998)

Van der Auwera and Plugian (1998: 80) proposed 'to use the term "modality" for those semantic domains that involve possibility and necessity as paradigmatic variants, that is, as constituting a paradigm with two possible choices, possibility and necessity.' This paradigm with possibility and necessity was taken to be the case in four semantic domains: i) participant-internal modality, ii) participant-external modality, iii) deontic modality, and iv) epistemic modality.

Participant-internal modality refers to 'a kind of possibility and necessity internal to the participant engaged in the state of affairs' (Van der Auwera and Plugian 1998: 80), as exemplified by (41). The term participant-external modality refers to 'circumstances that are external to the participant, if any, engaged in the state of affairs and that make this state of affairs either possible or necessary' (Van der Auwera and Plugian 1998: 80), as demonstrated in (42).

(41) [Participant-internal modality]
    a. *Boris can get by with sleeping five hours a night.*   [possibility]

b. *Boris* needs *to sleep ten hours every night for him to function properly.*
[necessity]

(42) [Participant-external modality]
    a. *To get to the station, you* can *take bus 66.*   [possibility]
    b. *To get to the station, you* have to *take bus 66.*   [necessity]

The term deontic modality refers to 'the enabling or compelling circumstances external to the participant as some person(s), often the speaker, and/or as some social or ethical norm (s) permitting or obliging the participant to engage in the state of affairs' (Van der Auwera and Plugian 1998: 81). The following is an example:

(43) a. *John* may *leave now.*
    b. *John* must *leave now.*

The term epistemic modality refers to 'a judgement of the speaker' (Van der Auwera and Plugian 1998: 81). In (44a), the speaker judges the uncertainty and possibility of the occurrence of the event. In (44b), the event is represented as relatively certain.[7]

(44) a. *John* may *have arrived.*
    b. *John* must *have arrived.*

Van der Auwera and Plugian (1998) arranged the paradigm for possibility and necessity in the four semantic dimensions presented below:

Table 2.5. Types of modality

Possibility			
Non-epistemic possibility			Epistemic possibility (Uncertainty)
Participant-internal Possibility (Dynamic possibility, Ability, Capacity)	Participant-external possibility		
	(Non-deontic possibility)	**Deontic possibility** (Permission)	
Participant-internal necessity (Need)	(Non-deontic possibility)	Deontic necessity (Obligation)	Epistemic necessity (Probability)
	Participant-external necessity		
Non-epistemic necessity			
Necessity			

(Van der Auwera and Plugian 1998: 82, bolds are mine)

Non-epistemic modality consists of participant-internal modality and participant-external modality. It concerns the 'aspect of an internal state of affairs that the proposition reflects,' while epistemic modality is concerned with 'the whole proposition' (cf. Van der Auwera and Plugian 1998: 81–82). Deontic modality is placed in the subcategory of participant-external modality because traditional terms like 'permission' and 'obligatory' fall under possibility or necessity depending on social or ethical norms.

In their discussion, as we can see from the following table, they only regarded inferential evidentiality as one of the subcategories of epistemic modality. That is, evidentiality is not completely separated from epistemic modality, but evidentiality and epistemic modality form a continuous relationship in which they partially overlap, as illustrated below:

Table 2.6. Inferential evidentiality = Epistemic necessity

		Necessity		
...	Deontic necessity	Epistemic necessity = Inferential evidentiality	Quotative evidentiality	...
		Evidentiality		

(Van der Auwera and Plugian 1998: 86)

2.5.3. De Haan (2001)

De Haan (2001:203) defined the difference between epistemic modality and evidentiality as follows: epistemic modality is a category related to possibility (weak epistemic modality) or necessity (strong epistemic modality), both of which represent 'the commitment of the speaker to the truth of what he/she is saying.' (De Haan 2001: 203), whereas evidentiality specifies the nature of the source of information on which the proposition of the speaker's statement is based. Van der Auwera and Plugian (1998) insisted that inference evidentials overlap with epistemic necessity, but De Haan (2001) was skeptical about this assertion. This is because English speakers can describe the same situation with different modalities such as those of epistemic necessity or possibility, or can even leave the sentence unmarked, as exemplified below:

(45) a. John must be at home. The light is on.

b. John may be at home. The light is on.
c. John is at home. The light is on.

(De Haan 2001: 208)

Thus, De Haan (2001) clearly distinguished evidentiality from epistemic modality. The former refers to the source of information of the speaker's statement, whereas the latter is concerned with the degree of commitment of the speaker to what they are saying.

2.5.4. The relation between modality and evidentiality: from the study of cognitive linguistics

The positions given in (39a) and (39b), both proposed by Palmer (1986, 2001) integrated evidentiality in a category of epistemic modality into the sense that both of them refer to the degree of commitment to what the speaker is saying. These positions define a unified category as a means of representing the speaker's unwillingness to present what they are saying as fact, so it could be said that the sensory parameter (cf. Aikhenvald 2004) is not included in this unified category. To avoid such a problem, the position (39c) proposed by Van der Auwera and Plugian (1998) conceived the idea that evidentials, specifically the inference parameter, partially overlapped with the modality that referred to epistemic necessity. However, as De Haan (2001) pointed out, the difficulty with the position is that this same situation can be described with or without different modalities (e.g. *John { must / may / ∅ } be at home. The light is on.*). In other words, it is questionable whether the inference parameter partially overlaps with the modality referring to epistemic necessity since various modalities can be used to describe this situation based on the same source of information.

I take a position similar to De Haan's (2001), positing that a proper distinction should be made between the categories of evidentiality and epistemic modality. My position is that the two categories operate complementarily when humans make a judgement or an epistemic assessment regarding the reality of the situation described by the speaker. Radden and Dirvan (2007: 235) assumed that our epistemic assessment requires three kinds of mental spaces. As shown in Figure 2.2, the mental space of the modal *must* refers to epistemic necessity. The example *There must be someone living in the house* prompts us to visualize three mental spaces: a reality space, in which the speaker has found some evidence of the house being lived in; a positive potentiality space of the house being lived in; and a negative potentiality space in which the house is uninhabited, a possibility which is excluded. The information regarding the three spaces is fed into the blended space represented in the epistemic assessment.

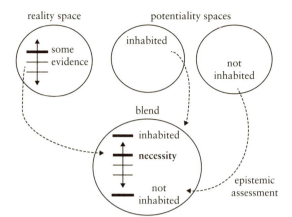

There must be someone living in the house.

(Radden and Dirvan 2007: 235)
Figure 2.2. Blending in epistemic assessment

Assuming that the judgement or epistemic assessment necessitates the process of blending these mental spaces, it is implied that the speaker using a modal expression has some evidence upon which their assessment of the probability of a situation relies. The difference between epistemic modality and evidentiality lies in whether or not the blended space that represents the epistemic assessment is focused on the reality space that shows the speaker's evidence.

In the modal statement (46a), the speaker makes an assessment regarding Peggy's sickness based on the paleness of her face. In this case, the focus is on the necessity expressed by the modal *must*, with any evidence for the statement being invoked as an implicature of the statement.[8] On the other hand, (46b) focuses on the basis for the speaker's assessment, with the judgement about her sickness being implied.

(46) a. Peggy must be sick. [*epistemic modality*]
    'the speaker has evidence for the claim' [*implicature*]
  b. Peggy looks pale. [*evidential assertion*]
    'Peggy's sickness is highly probable' [*implicature*]

(Radden and Dirvan 2007: 236)

As seen above, evidentiality and epistemic modality are cognitive functions that operate in complementary fashion to facilitate the determination of the reality of a given situation. When using evidentiality, the basis of the statement is what is focused on, whereas when using modal expression, the epistemic assessment is paramount. In Chapter 5, I will argue that the tendency to focus on one mental space or the others appears as a preference of construal, which depends on a difference in 'fashion of speaking' between English speakers and Japanese speakers (Ikegami 2011).

2.6. Mirativity

Delancey (2001) was the first to propose the semantic category of mirativity as distinct from evidentiality per se. In the words of Delancey (2001: 33), '[t]he fundamental function of this category is to mark sentences which report information which is new or surprising to the speaker.' According to Aikhenvald (2012), the following values are subsumed under the 'mirativity' label:

(47) *the 'mirativity' label*
    a. sudden discovery, sudden revelation or realization (a) by the speaker, (b) by the audience (or addressee), or (c) by the main character;
    b. surprise (a) of the speaker, (b) of the audience (or addressee), or (c) of the main character;
    c. unprepared mind (a) of the speaker, (b) of the audience (or addressee), or (c) of the main character;
    d. counter-expectation (a) to the speaker, (b) to the addressee, or (c) to the main character;
    e. information new (a) to the speaker, (b) to the addressee, or (c) to the main character.

(Aikhenvald 2012: 437)

Grammatical means of representing mirative meanings have been confirmed throughout the world. Additionally, according to Aikhenvald (2004: 219), markers that refer to indirect evidentials can develop mirative meanings as additional semantic overtones called 'first-person effect.'

(48) If one of the participants is 'I', a non-firsthand or a non-visual evidential may gain a range of additional meanings, to do with the first person participant not quite 'being all there'. Their actions are then interpreted as non-intentional, non-volitional, and generally lacking in control or awareness of what is happening. Not infrequently, these are linked to overtones of new information, unprepared mind, and surprise [...].

(Aikhenvald 2004: 220)

Indirect evidentiality represents information that the speaker obtains from the outer world. Thus, when an indirect evidential marker co-occurs with a first-person participant, this can imbue the sentence with added overtones of mirative meaning, expressing a contradictory situation in which the speaker is basing their statement on information gained from the outer world rather than on their own knowledge or experience.

In Jarawara, it is appropriate to use an indirect evidential marker in order to describe a situation where the speaker has no recollection of an event due to being hungover, as shown in (49b). On the other hand, a direct evidential marker is used in a case where the speaker can remember drinking and what they did the previous night, as exemplified by (49a).

(49) a. *o-hano-hara*   *o-ke.*
  1SG.S-be. drunk-IMM.P.FIRSTH.f 1SG-DECL.f
  'I got drunk (deliberately)' (FIRSTHAND)
 b. *o-hano-hani*   *o-ke.*
  1SG.S-be. drunk-IMM.P.NONFIRSTH.f 1SG-DECL.f
  'I got drunk (and don't recall it)' (NON-FIRSTHAND)

(Aikhenvald 2004: 221, glosses are mine)

As we observed above, there are two ways of expressing mirative meaning: in some cases it is coded as specific lexical and grammatical items, while in others it is expressed parasitically by grammatical items and constructions with no intrinsic mirative meaning. Peterson (2017) subdivided the possible ways of marking mirativity into four categories as follows.

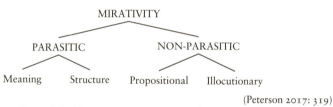

(Peterson 2017: 319)
Figure 2.3. (Non-)parasitic expressions of mirativity

Peterson (2017) divides mirative meanings into two major classes: a non-parasitic case where words or morphemes specifically encode mirative meanings, and a parasitic one where mirative meaning is not a part of the entailed meaning of the sentence. Words or morphemes in the non-parasitic case can be expressed without restriction of context. Expressions in the non-parasitic case are subdivided into a propositional type and an illocutionary type. The propositional type, as shown in (50), includes words or morphemes which are used to construct propositional[9] content. On the other hand, words encoded with mirative meaning at the speech act level were categorized as the illocutionary types such as (51).

(50) Chechen
   a. *Zaara   j-iena*
      Zara   j-come.PERF
      'Zara has come.' [and she is still here. I expected her to come]
   b. *Zaara   j-iena-q*
      Zara   j-come.PERF-MIR
      'Zara has come!' [I didn't expect her to come]

                                                            (Peterson 2017: 318)

(51) '**Wow, you made it!**'
    p = You made it

                                                            (Peterson 2017: 318)

The parasitic type, which includes words or constructions where mirative meanings are not encoded, is subcategorized into a meaning type and a structure type. The meaning type of parasitic meaning involves the use of a group of lexical or grammatical words which do not code mirative meanings intrinsically. The imperfective aspect marker *le* in sentence (52) expresses mirative meaning parasitically.

(52) Magar
    boi-e   chitua-ke   ngap-o   le
    father-ERG leopard-DAT shoot-NMLZ IMPF.MIR
    [I realise to my surprise that:] 'Father shot the leopard!'

                                                            (Peterson 2017: 316)

In the structure type, on the other hand, a set of constructions which do not code mirative meanings intrinsically can be used to represent mirative meaning parasitically. This is exemplified by (53b), where the *take*-V construction in Swedish represents the event with mirative overtones.

(53) Swedish
   a. *John   läste   en bok*
      John   read.PAST   a book
      'John read a book.'
   b. *John   tog   och   läste   en bok*
      John   take.PAST and   read.PAST a book
      [Surprisingly, unexpectedly, suddenly] 'John read a book.'

(Peterson 2017: 317–318)

The evidential -*rasi-i* I examine in Chapter 6 is defined as a form of indirect evidential marker in Japanese. If the evidential -*rasi-i* in combination with a first-person pronoun takes on mirative meaning in certain contexts, this mirative meaning is categorized as the structure type of the parasitic case. In other words, the meaning of evidential -*rasi-i* itself is inference or hearsay categorized as indirect evidentiality, but the construction comprised of evidential -*rasi-i* with a first-person pronoun can represent mirative meaning parasitically in the context where the speaker shows her own information obtained from the outer world.

2.7. What is at issue?

In this chapter, I have given an overview of evidentiality, including its parameters and how it is marked. I have clarified how previous studies have addressed the following three questions posed in Chapter 1:

I. What motivates the grammaticalization of evidential -*rasi-i* from its suffixal usage?
II. What is the difference between evidentiality and epistemic modality?
III. Why does mirative meaning arise when evidential -*rasi-i* is combined with first-person pronouns?

Regarding the first issue of the language change of evidential markers, we surveyed the source of evidential markers worldwide and the kinds of grammatical pathways through which they developed, based on Aikhenvald (2011). It is obvious that the language change of the Japanese evidential marker -*rasi-i* is a special case, having developed through yet a different path, namely from an adjective-forming suffix. For this reason, it can serve as valuable data from the perspective of typology. More importantly, the language change includes a structural change along with semantic and functional changes. Although some previous research on evidential -*rasi-i* from the perspective of Japanese linguistics (cf. Section. 4.2) has described the semantic transition from suffixal -*rasi-i* to evidential -*rasi-i* or from inference meaning to hearsay meaning, this has still not provided us with an adequate understanding of its language change. We need a study encompassing not only semantic but also structural change. In Chapter 4, I reveal the key factor driving the semantic and structural changes of evidential -*rasi-i* by incorporating the concept of the cycle of awakening which I present in Chapter 3.

I addressed the second issue above in Section 2.5, where I provided an overview of the three main positions on the relationship between evidentiality and epistemic modality, namely that they are to be viewed as: i) the same category, ii) partially overlapping categories, or iii) completely different categories. After surveying previous studies, I took the position that evidentiality and epistemic modality are cognitive functions operating complementarily to arrive at a judgement about the reality of the situation described. Supposing that they function complementarily, we have to make clear when and why each of them becomes the focus. In Chapter 5, I will approach the issue with data collected from novels written in both Japanese and English. I present examples where evidential -*rasi-i* in Japanese novels is rendered by English translation containing no words associated with evidentiality, and other examples where evidential -*rasi-i* appears in Japanese translation of an English original not containing such words. From the data, I will contend that the difference depends on a difference in 'fashion of speaking', namely subjective construal vs objective construal (cf. Section 5.2.2).

In Section 2.6, in connection with the third issue, I reviewed the definition of mirativity and the first-person effect of evidentiality, referring mainly to Aikhenvald (2011). Considered in light of the basic claim of cognitive linguistics, mirativity is not a conception defined morpho-syntactically or by logical semantics but a general cognitive phenomenon. My proposal is that mirativity is a reconstruction of the conceptualizer's own reality caused by an interaction with their environment or with others. In Chapter 6, I will demonstrate how the mirative meaning of evidential -*rasi-i* can be derived through the implication of additional meaning of evidentiality in combination with first-person pronoun.

Notes
1 The term 'everything else' represents unmarked members expressing evidential neutrality.
2 Traditionally, scholars included '-*to i-u*' and '-*tte*' as evidential markers denoting the hearsay parameter, but according to the criteria of Aikhenvald (2004), they are treated as part of the quotative parameter.
3 When the evidential -*soo=da* represents the inference parameter, it is regarded as a suffixal usage because it follows a verb or adjective stem (cf. NKBK 2003: 170).
4 Kinoshita (1998) divided inference into deductive inference and inductive inference and regarded the inference encoded by Japanese evidential markers as inductive inference. Technically speaking, inductive inference is a method of reasoning in which some commonality is abstracted from supplied instances to reach a conclusion of truth. The inference parameter of evidentiality represents reasoning that extrapolates the cause from observed phenomena, so it is reasonable to suppose that the inference parameter of evidentiality denotes abductive reasoning.

5 Miyake (1994) pointed out that we cannot read a sentence with evidential -*rasi-i* as the hearsay evidential in a context such as a monologue, while the evidential -*soo=da* representing the hearsay evidential can be used in such a context. (e.g. [in the context of a monologue] *mata en=ga saga-tte, 1 yuuro=ga 200 yen=ni nat-ta* {#-*soo=da* / -*rasi-i*}'It is seemed that the Japanese yen fell again to 200 yen per Euro.').
6 There is little difference between positions a and b, and for that reason, I bundled them together in a group.
7 The term 'relatively certain' concerns necessity as shown below:
   This concerns necessity, for relative to some judgments (e.g., the belief that when John comes by bike, he chains his bike to the tree and the belief that the bike is in fact chained to the tree right now) John's arrival is necessary.   (Van der Auwera and Plugian 1998: 81)
8 Radden and Dirvan (2007) defined evidential meaning as an implicature of the statement when the modal was expressed. However, the evidential meaning should be regarded as presupposition because it is doubtful that the meaning can be cancelled. For example, the expression *Peggy must be sick* is based on the speaker's evidence (e.g. The speaker saw Peggy's sickly pale face). In this case, the evidence was presupposed to judge the truth condition of the proposition (i.e. Peggy is sick or not). Therefore, speaker's judgement of the truth condition is contradictory if the evidence cannot be cancelled by a statement *Peggy must be sick but I don't have any evidence*.
9 Peterson (2017: 7) took the term *propositional* 'to describe meaning that is entailed.'

CHAPTER 3
The concept of subjectivity in cognitive grammar

3.1. Introduction

Cognitive grammar (CG) claims that language is symbolic in nature and that meaning is equated with conceptualization. In other words, human linguistic ability is based on general cognitive ability. The following conceptual substrate, called 'viewing arrangement' — where the subject of conception (S) construes its object of conception (O) — lies at the foundation of CG theory. In the full scope of awareness, S pays attention to a certain region called the onstage region, in which the object of conception is focused on. 'To the extent that the situation is polarized, we can say that S is construed *subjectively* and O *objectively*' (Langacker 2008: 260).

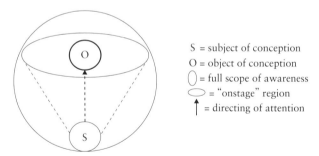

(Langacker 2008: 260)

Figure 3.1. Conceptual substrate

The roles of S and O are two facets of conceptualizing, but the relationship is asymmetrical. The O profiled in the onstage region is encoded, while the S engages in conceptualizing activity and is the locus of conceptual experience. Langacker (1990) distinguished three classes of degree of subjectivity reflected in expressions. The ground (G) is used in CG to indicate a speech event that includes its participant (speaker and hearer), their interaction, and the immediate circumstances (the time and place of speaking) (Langacker 2008: 259). Since the speaker and hearer in the ground are participants who express and understand their conception of what is encoded in their speech, they are equated with the subject of conception in Figure 3.1.[1] The degree of subjectivity is dependent on the scope of predication that the ground is placed in. An expression's maximal scope (MS) is the full extent of its coverage, where no entity is profiled, i.e. the scope is not the range designated directly. The limited immediate scope (IS) is the most objectively construed region where the profiled entity (in the bold line) is posited.

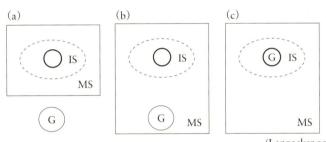

(Langacker 1990: 319)

Figure 3.2. Degree of subjectivity

The difference between Figure 3.2 (a) and Figure 3.2 (b) lies in whether G is external to the MS as a subject that engages in conceptualization or whether it remains within the MS as an implicit, unprofiled reference point.[2] The class represented by Figure 3.2 (a) is comprised of lexical items such as *dog*, *boy*, and *like*, where G is construed most subjectively as the subject of conceptualization, being external to the objectively construed range directly related to linguistic expression. The class represented by Configuration (b) subsumes expressions related to deixis, such as certain lexical words (e.g. *tomorrow*: the day after the speech event) and grounding expressions that implicitly refer to the relationship between the ground and profiled entities (e.g. demonstratives: *this/that*; articles: *a boy/the boy*; tense and modalities: *He {likes/liked/will like} a dog.*). In this configuration, G is incorporated in the MS as a reference point of the expression, where the designated event is described in relation to G.[3] Thus the conception of time must be understood in relation to the time of speaking, and the conception of distance such as *this vs. that* from the standpoint of G in space. Figure 3.2 (c) is the configuration comprised of expressions that directly refer to an element in G such as *I*, *here*, or *now*.

What should concern us here is that the two scopes——the MS and the IS——are the regions where the subject of conception is conscious of its own awareness. Thus, the subject conceptualizing the configuration in Figure 3.2

exists external to the MS and is separate from the conceptualizer. That is, the G in the MS is conceptualized only as a reference point for placing profiled entities in relation to the ground. In the framework of subjectivity proposed by Langacker, an increase in subjectivity depends on whether the conceptualizer becomes conscious of himself and his construal as the object of conception and to what extent the conceptualizer realizes his own cognitive process meta-cognitively.

3.2. Subjectification

Langacker's subjectivity is the degree to which the subject of conception (i.e. conceptualizer) incorporates their consciousness into the conception encoded by linguistic expressions. In the case of lexical items where the conceptualizer is construed most subjectively, the conceptualizer is external to the expression of the MS (cf. Figure 3.2.(a)). This means that lexical items reflect the configuration where 'the ground's involvement goes beyond this minimal presence' (Langacker 2008: 262). In the case of grammatical elements related to deixis, such as tense and modality, the ground is placed in the MS or IS as a reference point to posit the profiled entities in light of time, reality, or space. Therefore, subjects of conception are conscious of themselves as the point in relation to which the object of conception is placed (cf. Figure 3.2 (b)).

The framework of subjectivity is used in various fields such as language change and comparative language studies. In this book, I focus on 'subjectification' (Langacker 1985, 1991, 1999b) as a process of language change. Langacker (1991: 215) defined subjectification as a semantic shift or extension in which an entity originally construed objectively comes to receive a more subjective construal. Langacker posited two types of subjectification. One is exemplified in (1) and the other in (2). In both cases, (a) is more subjective than (b) (Langacker 1990: 326, 328).

(1) a. Vanessa jumped across the table.
    b. Vanessa is sitting across the table from Veronika.

(2) a. Vanessa is sitting across the table from me.
    b. Vanessa is sitting across the table.

The use of the preposition *across* in (1a–b) represents an example of 'subjectification due to attenuation.' As shown by (3), this type of subjectification is a semantic change caused by attenuation of the objective content that is immanent in the word. Consequently, the subjective construal that is inherent in the original lexical meanings is laid bare.

(3) An *objective* relationship fades away, leaving behind a *subjective* relationship that was originally *immanent* in it (i.e. inherent in its conceptualization).

(Langacker 1999b: 77)

In (1a), *across* designates an objective motion of trajector (tr), defining a path leading from one side of the landmark (lm) to the other. In (1b), the objective motion is attenuated and the conceptualizer's mental tracing of the path from Veronika to Vanessa remains. It is important that this semantic change is not a shift from objective motion to mental tracing, but a retention of the mental scanning caused by the fading away of objective motion. The semantic change is diagramed in Figure 3.3 (a–c). Through time, represented by the solid arrow (t), the objective movement of the trajector (Vanessa) is described using a continuous series of circles through time. In Figure 3.3 (b), the series of circles from Figure 3.3 (a) has faded away, being replaced by a broken arrow instead, which demonstrates the attenuation of objective motion. Both of the figures depict broken lines being emitted from G, illustrating the conceptualizer's mental scanning.

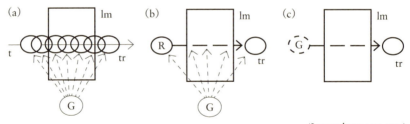

(Langacker 1990: 327)

Figure 3.3. Subjectification due to attenuation

The second type of subjectification is related to the conceptualizer's vantage point, as exemplified by (2). In sentence (2a), the speaker (G) refers to herself using *from me*, because the relationship between Vanessa and the speaker is described by the speaker from a third person perspective. On the other hand, the speaker of sentence (2b) designates herself implicitly, insomuch that the sentence describes a situation where the speaker sees Vanessa in front of her. The difference between the two sentences is illustrated in Figure 3.3 (b–c). While the speaker (G) employs the reference point (R) designated by the term *from me* in order to locate the trajector (Vanessa) (tr) vis-à-vis the reference point, in Figure 3.3(c) G's vantage point is moved to the position occupied by the reference point (R) in Figure 3.3 (b) to indicate that the speaker is in the onstage region and is thus construed more objectively. The difference between the two sentences is illustrated in Figure 3.3 (b–c). The objective construal of the speaker in the onstage region means the expression receives greater subjective meaning in Langacker's theory of subjectivity since the speaker is placed in their own field of awareness.

Langacker (2008, 2011) also regarded the following phenomenon as a case of subjectification, one I term 'subjectification caused by disengaged cognition.' It is a process whereby an operation originally applied by conceptualizers to formulate an objective circumstance come to be independent of that objective circumstance, thus becoming a new tool to construe the world.

(4) In a final means of transcending direct experience, mental operations inherent in a certain kind of experience are applied to situations with respect to which their occurrence is extrinsic. This is called **subjectification**, indicating that the operations come to be independent of the objective circumstances where they initially occur and whose apprehension they partially constitute.

(Langacker 2008: 528)

For example, the nominal phrase *a broken vase* evokes the resultative state of the vase being broken. Not every use of the participle *broken* implies an actual change, however. The nominal phrase *a broken line* uses the same participle though it does not describe any actual process of breaking, designating instead only a kind of line. In this case, the mental operation originally inherent in the process of breaking (e.g. a mental operation for understanding the shattering of something) is independent of any situation described as an actual change of state, for it is merely applied to describe the line's shape. Although this kind of subjectification is seemingly irrelevant to other kinds, the objective conception is bleached out and the construal for comprehending the objective scene (a broken thing) is independent of it. Thus, we can say that this subjectification is an alternative explanation of the aforementioned 'subjectification due to attenuation.'

3.3. Grounding and layering

Grounding is one of the most important frameworks intimately related to subjectivity. Grounding is a semantic function that establishes 'the location vis-à-vis the ground of the thing or process serving as the nominal or clausal profile' (Langacker 1991: 549). Elements that specify the grounding status are called grounding elements. English has two types of grounding systems: nominal grounding and clausal grounding. Since a noun profiles a thing or an object and 'the default expectation for objects is that they will continue to exist unless something happens to change their state' (Langacker 2009: 150), nominal grounding serves as a function that identifies the thing that the speaker and listener on the ground are talking about. The nominal grounding elements are comprised of demonstratives, articles, and relative quantifiers (e.g. *each*, *every*, *any*). In clausal grounding, the issue is not the identification of the profiled entity, but its occurrence. In other words, clausal grounding seeks to ascertain whether the event that is spoken about actually occurs. Thus, 'the clausal grounding situates the profiled relationship with respect to the speaker's current conception of reality' (Langacker 2008: 259). Elements like tense and modality, which designate such functions, are considered to be clausal grounding elements.

The typical grounding relationship is illustrated in Figure 3.3. The ground (G) consists of the speaker (S), the hearer (H), and their interaction in the context (double-headed broken arrow). The rectangle labeled as OS (onstage region) —— also referred to as or IS (immediate scope) —— is the region where the profiled entity (bold circle and arrow) is placed. The outer rectangle, composed of the OS and G, represents the MS (maximal scope). This configuration is the same as in Figure 3.2 (b).

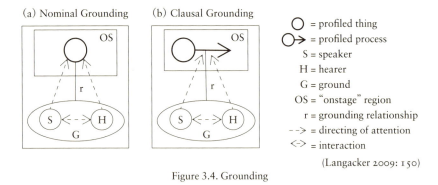

Figure 3.4. Grounding

What is represented by the grounding element is primarily schematic nominal and finite clauses rather than lexical elements. While the latter may enter into the representation, it is the former that are the focus of the grounding element. And the configuration representing such schematic nominal and finite clauses is more subjective than that representing lexical elements. Only the grounded entity is profiled, whereas other components such as G and the grounding relationship between the grounded entity and G are unprofiled and encoded implicitly. Thus, this configuration shows that the expression with grounding elements has G as the reference point to posit the objective conception designated by the noun or clause.

As noted above, the clausal grounding system is related to the occurrence of events that are referred to by finite clauses. Clausal grounding has two components: immediacy, which pertains to the epistemic distance between an event and G; and reality, which is related to the truthfulness of an event designated by a proposition. The degree of immediacy is determined by either the presence or absence of a marker. Likewise, reality is determined by the presence or absence of modality.

		Modality	
Distance	φ	*may, can, will, shall, must*	Immediate
	-ed	*might, could, would, should*	Non-Immediate
	Real	Unreal	

Figure 3.5. Clausal grounding

(Langacker 2009: 162)

Both tense and modals are highly grammaticalized in English and entrenched in the grammatical system, constituting finite clauses. Such grounding elements that function as finite clauses are called 'clause-internal grounding elements.'

The conception of reality proposed by Langacker (2008, 2009) is based on the 'control cycle' (Langacker 2002). The control cycle is a general cognitive model that is inherent in and abstracted from many aspects of experience. It is a cyclic process involving striving for control and 'manifestations of the control cycle continuously unfold at the physical, perceptual, mental, and social levels' (Langacker 2009: 130). The control cycle at the epistemic level is related to knowledge of events and propositions. Langacker (2009) applied it to the analysis of modality, representing the presence and absence of modals as in Figure 3.6, where C is the conceptualizer, P the target proposition, and D (epistemic dominion) the conceptualizer's current conception of reality. The presence of a modal verb is understood to constitute the inclination phase, where C inclines toward accepting P as part of C's view of reality. Its absence constitutes the result phase, where the P is already established in C's dominion. The traditional terms possibility and necessity can be rendered in several different ways, and the length of the arrow represents C's commitment to the proposition.

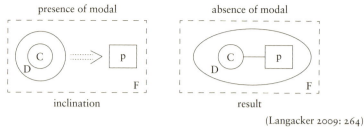

Figure 3.6. Reality model

(Langacker 2009: 264)

(5) a. She { may / might / could / should / will / must } be upset. [inclination]
    b. She {is / was } upset. [result]

(Langacker 2009: 264)

Although cognitive grammar regards tense and modality in verbs as clausal grounding elements, Langacker (2009) stated that the matrix clauses of complementation (e.g. *Joe believes* they will finish the project on time.) and modal adverbials (e.g. *Perhaps* they will finish the project.) also serve the function of grounding. With respect to complementation, as is the case with a clausal-internal grounding system, the semantic description of matrix predicates represents whether or not P is established in C's reality, as exemplified by (6). The epistemic control cycle can also be represented by elements external to finite clauses. These are called 'clause-external grounding elements.'

(6) a. **Inclination:** I { suspect / believe / suppose / think / Figure / reckon } they will never agree to my offer.
    b. **Result:** He { knows / believes / thinks / realizes / accepts / is sure / is certain / is convinced} that Bush is a pacifist.

(Langacker 2009: 132)

As is also the case with complementation and modal adverbials, the layering structure of clausal-external grounding mirrors that of clausal-internal grounding, the two levels being essentially the same. However, there are also some crucial differences. One is the nature of the target. In the clause-internal grounding shown in Figure 3.7(a), the target is the profiled process represented by **p**, whereas in the clause-external grounding in Figure 3.7(b–c), it is the proposition (**P**) expressed by the finite complement clause. In CG theory, propositions designated by finite clauses are defined as processes grounded by the conceptualizer that reside in the grounding element of the finite clauses. Another difference is related to the profiling of C. With complementation, the clausal subject in the matrix clause is profiled because the matrix predicate refers to the subject's commitment to the target proposition designated by the complement clause and the overtly marked subject is a conceptualizer who assesses the reality of the proposition. This configuration was shown in Figure 3.7 (b) by a profiled C and a bold arrow emitting from C. With modal adverbials, only C's assessment, which is depicted as a bold arrow, is profiled, with C itself remaining unprofiled, as shown in Figure 3.7 (c). This is because the modal adverbial overtly marks C's commitment to the proposition but does not overtly mark its conceptualizer (cf. Langacker 2009: Ch.9).

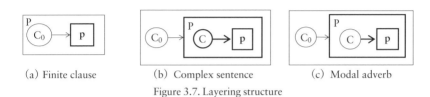

(a) Finite clause   (b) Complex sentence   (c) Modal adverb

Figure 3.7. Layering structure

As seen above, the relationship between clause-internal and clause-external grounding comprises a layered structure in which the clause-internal grounding [G⇒p] is contained within the clause-external grounding [G⇒P[G⇒p]]. This structure is required to theoretically explain the higher levels of organization at which the grounding relationship is duplicated. With the complementation exemplified in (7), the ground designated by the underlined clause with tense and modal is not the actual speech event, but rather the speech event including a third person denoted as the subject in the matrix clause (7a) or as the one who conveys the information to the speaker (7b–c). In this way, the conceptualizer invoked by the clausal element is not always identified as the actual speaker. 'It is thus a virtual (or imagined) conceptualizer unless and until it comes to be identified with a specific individual' (Langacker 2009: 232). By default, it is equated with the actual speaker. In this way, we need to assume a layering structure like that shown above in order to distinguish the assessment of the virtual conceptualizer from the assessment of the actual speaker.

(7) a. Jack says [that <u>Jill **may** be waiting for us</u>]—but I know for a fact that she isn't.
b. Conceivably <u>Jill **is** waiting for us</u>—but I really doubt it.
c. <u>Jill **is** waiting for us</u>. Well, you can say that, but I don't believe it.

(Langacker 2009: 231)

3.4. De-subjectification

Langacker's analysis is based on the conceptual substrate where a subject of conception construes an object of conception (Figure 3.1). Strictly speaking, concerning the relationship between perception and cognition, we can distinguish two positions: 'conceptualism' and 'non-conceptualism' (cf. Noya 2016). Non-conceptualism claims that people regard a perceptual activity before conceptualization, and that there is a process of leading from this act of perception to a cognition of the world. In particular, when we perceive a stimulus from the environment, we recognize what kind of entity the obtained information is categorized into. The problem with non-conceptualism, however, is that it cannot explain why the same stimulus can give rise to several different conceptions. For example, in perceiving the figure called 'Rubin's vase,' the same stimulus can be recognized as two different conceptions: a vase or a pair of faces. In other words, the perception of the same stimulus does not always translate to the same conception. To explain this phenomenon, the 'non-conceptualist' position is forced to admit that preconceptions exist prior to the perception of an object in the environment.

Figure 3.8. The reversible figure 'Rubin's vase'

On the other hand, conceptualism insists that we cannot see things that we do not have a conception of because we only perceive the world through our own conceptions. In other words, according to conceptualism, we do not perceive a cat, but instead perceive a certain object (X) as our conception of a cat. The problem with conceptualism, however, is that our conceptions are inconsistent. When we encounter an unknown entity, we can perceive and recognize it in accordance with conceptions that are already known to us. This means that we receive stimuli from the environment around us and these stimuli significantly affect the formation and adjustment of our conceptions. In my opinion, it is not imperative to choose between either one of these two extreme views. In fact, it is appropriate to consider the two opposite positions to be complementary. That is, though we perceive the world through our own conceptions, our embodied interaction with the environment is the force that facilitates the

CHAPTER 3 THE CONCEPT OF SUBJECTIVITY IN COGNITIVE GRAMMAR 45

expansion and adjustment of our existing conceptions in order to reconstruct applicable conceptions for novel entities. Given this assumption, human cognition is a conceptualizing activity that involves a cycle of collapsing and reconstructing conceptions through our experiential interaction with the environment around us.

Langacker (2008: Ch.14) also pointed out the importance of embodied cognition. Our conception is formed on the basis of our directly embodied interaction with the world, such as our sensory and motor experiences. Conceptions are abstracted through the repetition of experiences and established as 'simulations.' The process of converting a direct physical experience into disengaged cognition is illustrated in Figure 3.9. As shown in Figure 3.9 (a), we directly interact with something in the world (W) and recognize the world inclusive of the entity through direct experience. The interaction (double arrow) is effected through our body via our sensory and motor organs. The box labeled A represents the role of the brain, which conducts the processing activity that constitutes the interactive experience. By experiencing the same event at different times, we can distinguish between comparable processes without the embodied interaction: a 'certain facet of A —— labeled A' —— comes to occur automatically, in the absence of any current interaction with W' (Langacker 2008: 536), where A indicates the brain activity that constitutes the interactive experience, and A' the simulation abstracted from this activity.

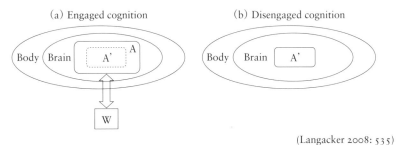

Figure 3.9. Embodied cognition
(Langacker 2008: 535)

In various fields and under different labels, simulation is understood to play a fundamental role in conceptualization. The simulation is grounded not in a specific sensory organ, but rather in multi-modal simulations that occur as a pattern of neural firing in various modalities (e.g. visual, auditory, and tactile systems) when we interact with certain entities (cf. Barsalou 1983). When babies recognize someone as their mother, they receive pertinent information through multimodal neural networks, which they store accordingly. This information includes a visual image of their mother, an auditory image (such as her voice), and a tactile image (such as her texture). Afterward, when babies see their mother again and again, their neural networks react to the stimulus and are activated simultaneously. Therefore, the simulation 'mother' is entrenched in their category, and they can conjure up an image of their mother without any perceptual stimulation. Thus, assuming this theory of cognition, our conceptualization of some entity is a kind of reenactment of its simulation once we have interacted with it and the environment around it. This conceptualization on the basis of embodied interaction is quite useful for analyzing the expansions of lexical meanings. For example, assuming that the lexical word *lemon* represents not just the fruit but also comprises the simulation in which one directly experiences the fruit's sour taste, it can be logically extended to metaphorically mean 'defective' (e.g. *The car we bought is a lemon.*). The simulation occurring when we receive the embodied experience of sourness through our direct interaction with a lemon is projected metaphorically onto our experience of being suckered into buying a defective item. This semantic change is allowed because our embodied interactions with the world reside in our conceptualizations.

Nakamura (2009, 2012, 2016, 2019) proposed a framework called 'the mode of cognition' to incorporate an aspect of such embodied cognition into CG theory. Nakamura (2016) assumed two types of cognitive modes. In the first, called the 'interactional mode of cognition, or I-mode' and shown in Figure 3.10, we construct a cognitive image (③) through our interaction (①double headed arrow) with the environment and construe the object (② broken arrow) in the domain of cognition (the range depicted as an ellipse). In the other, called the 'Displaced mode of cognition, or D-mode,' we are displaced from the domain of cognition and face off against the object of conception to recognize it analytically (Nakamura 2016: 32-33).

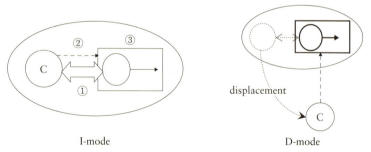

Figure 3.10. The mode of cognition

According to Nakamura (2009, 2016, 2019), Langacker's viewing arrangement is formed by a process of displacement (i.e. de-subjectification). We directly interact with a thing in our environment and form a cognitive image of it, which then is observed by a conceptualizer external to the domain of cognition as if it had previously existed.

Japanese mental predicates such as *samu-i* 'feel cold' reflect I-mode cognition because the subject of a sentence with a mental predicate is restricted to the first-person (e.g. *{Watasi / ??Kare}=wa samu-i!* '{I / he} is cold!'). Mental predicates are utilized to describe the direct experience of the speaker without any analytical view of the situation, the subject and object of conception being regarded as undifferentiated. In the case where the speaker says *Samu-i!* after leaving the house, the expression conflates two different meanings: 'the speaker feels cold' and 'the temperature around the speaker is cold.' Thus, the I-mode is a cognitive process that facilitates the formation of a viewing arrangement. In other words, the asymmetric configuration of subject versus object of conception is created based on the I-mode of cognition. In this respect, the I-mode differs from Figure 3.2(c), which Langacker defined as an egocentric viewing arrangement where the vantage point is posited inside the situation (i.e. inside IS, or MS).

From the viewpoint of mode of cognition, Nakamura (2016) defines our conception of reality as follows:

(8) If we regard a situation as a cognitive image constructed through the I-mode cognition, we treat the situation as irreal, on the other hand, if we perceive a situation without a process of constructing a cognitive image through the I-mode cognition (i.e. the situation just perceived in D-mode cognition), we treat the situation as real.

(Nakamura 2016: 35)

Taking 'the sun rises' as an example, it was a moral certainty for medieval people who believed in the Ptolemaic theory. However, when the Copernican theory overturned their common assumption that the sun revolves around the earth, they realized what they had taken to be real was in fact an illusion. The Copernican Revolution transformed their prior belief from real to irreal. To accept the new fact that the rising of the sun merely appears to be real, they needed D-mode cognition in which they employed analytical and scientific thinking. Thus, if a given situation is conceptualized against the background of I-mode cognition, in which we construct our own cognitive image, then the situation is regarded as irreal, whereas if it is conceptualized from a scientific view that does not utilize I-mode cognition, then the situation is treated as real.

3.5. The cycle of awakening

In this book, I will focus on conceptualization as a cycle of collapse and reconstruction through our embodied interaction with the environment, rather than using Langacker's configuration of conceptualization, where the subject of conception construes the object of conception. In order to refine the analysis of evidentiality, I will in this section incorporate the arguments of Sadanobu (2008) and Noya (1999, 2016) with the mode of cognition proposed by Nakamura (2009, 2016, 2019), and go on to introduce my own framework, called 'the cycle of awakening.'

The information related to 'experience' presented by Sadanobu (2008) is parallel to 'the interaction with the environment,' the significance of which was highlighted by Nakamura (2016, 2019). Sadanobu (2008) claimed that the information designated by languages is divided into that based on 'experience' and that based on 'knowledge.' While information based on 'knowledge' can be shared with other people, information based on the speaker's own 'experience' can either not be shared at all or shared only with a limited few. The two categories form a continuum correlated with the degree of 'shareability,' as shown below:

(Sadanobu 2008: 185)
Figure 3.11. Information of knowledge and experience

Sentence (9a) conveys information based on knowledge shared by many people, whereas (9b) is a sentence uttered by an astronaut after returning from outer space.

(9) a. *Genzai=wa   ao-i=ga,   taiko=no   mukasi=wa   tikyuu=wa*
    presence=TOP   blue-NPST=CONC   ancient=GEN   backward=TOP   earth=TOP
    aka-kat-ta.   [Knowledge]
    red-VBLZ-PST
    '[I have knowledge that] At present the earth is blue, but in times immemorial the earth was red.'

   b. *Kikan-suru toki,   utyuu=o   mi-ta=ra   nazeka   tikyuu=wa*
    return-VS time   space=OBJ   see-PST=COND   somehow   earth=TOP
    aka-kat-ta.   [Experience]
    red-VBLZ-PST
    'I saw the earth when I was in outer space, and somehow the earth looked red.'

Since sentence (9a) is based on knowledge, we can argue whether the proposition 'in times immemorial the earth was red' is true or not. However, the only people who can discuss the veracity of sentence (9b), which is based on experiential information, is the speaker himself or the individuals who were also present when the event occurred. In this sense, knowledge-based information is shared with many, while experience-based information is shared with a limited few.

As we can see from (9), both types of information are regarded as real because neither sentence contains any markers such as modals that represent the event as irreal. However, the nature of the reality is quite different in the two cases. The reality of the knowledge-based information is mutually accepted and shared with others intersubjectively, while the reality of experience-based information is created and held by the speaker alone. So, at what point in the scale do we begin to feel that the event is irreal? It is in the phase where we are in an unstable condition due to the collapse of our own reality.

In connection with the argument presented by Sadanobu (2008), 'aspect seeing'[4] in Wittgenstein's later works is deeply related to the cycle of reality that I focus on. 'Aspect seeing' is the ability to see one thing in a new light. It can be formulated as 'X looks like Y.' This awakening to a new aspect is a cyclic process, as demonstrated below:

(10) First phase: single perspective
     Second phase: multiple perspectives (unstable)
     Third phase: multiple perspectives (stable)

In the first phase, we unthinkingly perceive entities which we come across in the world from a single perspective. The stable phase where a referent is undoubtedly associated with its aspect is the first stage 'single perspective' (cf. Noya 1999). When we wake up to another aspect of the referent upon recognizing its similarity to another object or becoming cognizant of different views that others have of it, we move into the second 'multiple perspectives (unstable)' phase. This phase is unstable because we cannot determine which aspect is appropriate to the referent and are thus confused about how its reality is to be conceived. This unstable phase ends when the new aspect of the referent is shared with others and entrenched in their conception of reality, and then the shift to the third 'multiple perspectives (stable)' phase occurs.[5] For instance, in a situation where children are playing house with their mother, if the children use a rock to signify a rice ball, their mother moves into the unstable second phase because she is initially unsure as to why they are equating the rock with a rice ball. By talking to her children, she would further understand their manner of play and similarly utilize the rock to signify a rice ball. Thus, they will develop a shared understanding and consolidate the manner in which they playhouse together. The context that is established by sharing a new aspect of the referent is the third 'multiple perspective (stable)' phase. Integrating this aspect of seeing into the shareability scale of information gives us a new perspective on the conception of reality. Experience-based information is conceived of as real by the conceptualizer who has obtained the information. Knowledge-based information is also considered as real because the information is established as common sense by a broader number of people. Most importantly, the conception of irreality arises when the conceptualizer's own reality based on experience-based information conflicts with the conventionalized reality (i.e. knowledge-based information). This conflict between experience-based and knowledge-based information gives rise to confusion as to us the reality of the situation. The conceptualizer consequently conceptualizes the situation as irreal with uncertainty. In addition, a perception gap between conceptualizers forces them to conceptualize the situation as irreal because they cannot share any common understanding of the reality of the situation.

Based on this discussion above, I will present my framework 'the cycle of awakening' (illustrated in Figure 3.12) to facilitate my analysis of the conception of reality as a cycle of collapse and reconstruction through our embodied interaction with the environment. Figure 3.12 (a) illustrates our daily experience, where we unthinkingly perceive entities we come across in the world and accept them as part of the natural order on an unconscious level (e.g. we can walk with little awareness of the complex physical movements involved, such as which foot to take the first step with). This phase represents I-mode cognition, in which the subject and object of conception are still not separated and where we are not conscious of the realness of the entities.[6] In encountering new situations, it is common for us to construe them by using conceptions different from those we normally employ in our daily lives. In this context, the world that we are familiar with overlaps with a new world that we observe scientifically, as illustrated in Figure 3.12 (b).

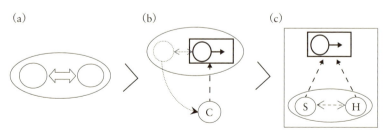

Figure 3.12. The cycle of awakening

Discerning a new aspect of the referent consists of two facets of cognition. One is the collapse of ready-made conceptions or stereotypes, whereas the other is the rebuilding of conception to comprehend an unknown phenomenon by adjusting the conceptions that we already possess. Although we temporarily experience an unstable state and lose sight of reality, the epistemic coordination of aspects conceptualized by others fixes the unstable state, as depicted in Fig 3.12(c). According to the usage-based theory in cognitive linguistics (cf. Tomasello 1999, 2003), a novel expression and the construal (or conceptualization) designated by it emerges from usage. Thus, the structure and meaning are shared with others and entrenched in the language community through our daily language usage. My theory is parallel to this usage-based theory, but it also accounts for the collapse of ready-made conceptions. This facet is extremely crucial when considering how our conception of reality is generated.

3.6. Summary

In this chapter, I introduced frameworks for examining and understanding evidential *-rasi-i*. The conceptual substrate in CG is the subject-object arrangement shown in Figure 3.1. Although this book fundamentally adheres to the argument of subjectivity proposed by Langacker, in order to describe the cognitive process of evidential *-rasi-i*, I incorporated the mode of cognition proposed by Nakamura (2016) and propounded my own framework, called the cycle of awakening. In subsequent chapters, I employ this framework to address the three issues regarding evidential *-rasi-i*, raised in Chapter 2. In Chapter 4, I deal with the issue of language change, arguing for a holistic approach to the constructional and semantic changes undergone by evidential *-rasi-i* over time. An explanation of the constructional changes requires an understanding of subjectification and layering structure, concepts introduced in Sections 3.2 and 3.3 respectively. In addition, its constructional change is closely related to its semantic change, in that it can be described as a transition from knowledge-based information to experiential information (cf. Figure 3.11). In Chapter 5, I explore the differences between Japanese and English in the ways they prefer to express evidentiality, citing data taken from novels. I conclude that when Japanese evidential *-rasi-i* is used in novels, the situation described is construed experientially as if the storyteller were in the narrative world, whereas English speakers tend not to describe the situation using that way of construal. In Chapter 6, I discuss the mirative extension of evidential *-rasi-i*, which implies an additional meaning of evidentiality in combination with first-person pronouns. Assuming that the cycle of awakening is reflected in evidential *-rasi-i*, the mirative extension is reasonably explained by adding the difference of profiling⁷. Thus, a conceptualizer which interacts with an object is profiled to express mirative meaning, while an object with which a conceptualizer interacts is profiled to express evidential meaning.

Notes

1 The ground (G) is not always identified with the conceptualizer. (see Layering in Section 3.5 of this volume).
2 Reference point ability is a fundamental capacity 'to invoke one conceived entity (a *reference point*) for the purpose of establishing mental contact with another (the *target*)' (Langacker 1991: 552).
3 Configuration (b) does not necessarily represent only a grounding relationship. It can only do if the objective content in the configuration could be construed schematically.
4 In his late works Wittgenstein's states that the aspect seeing is based on family resemblance.
5 The conception in stable multi-perspectives leads to a new single perspective by regarding the conception as a shared one and entrenching it in the conceptualizer's mental universe.
6 A state in which real and irreal are not distinguished would be a disputed situation. When we start to walk, for example, we automatically take our first step with one foot or the other without even being aware of it.
7 Profile is defined as 'the entity that an expression designates. A substructure within its base that is obligatorily accessed, accorded special prominence, and functions as the focal point within the immediate scope predication.' (Langacker 1991: 551)

CHAPTER 4

The language change of Japanese evidential -*rasi-i*

4.1. Introduction

As observed in Section 2.4, from the perspective of typological studies, two types of grammatical pathways were confirmed: i) the traditional grammaticalization path, in which grammatical evidentials developed through the grammaticalization of lexical items, and ii) the evidentiality strategy path, wherein essentially non-evidential forms acquire evidential status in their own right. However, neither of these paths are suitable to explain the language change of the Japanese evidential -*rasi-i*, which developed from the suffix -*rasi-i*. In Japanese linguistics as well, there has been little comprehensive study of both its semantic and constructional changes. In this chapter, I overview previous research on Japanese evidential -*rasi-i* and highlight the problems with it. After that, I summarize its historical transformation to clarify the evolution of the grammatical evidential marker -*rasi-i*. Finally, I identify the key cognitive factor driving the language change.

The language change of evidential -*rasi-i* is characterized by both semantic and constructional changes. Specifically, suffixal -*rasi-i* with a preceding noun developed into evidential -*rasi-i* with a preceding finite clause. What drives the constructional change is rebracketing from a suffixal construction [A=*wa* [X]-*rasi-i*] into an evidential construction [[A=*wa* X]-*rasi-i*]. This constructional change is closely related to a semantic change, in which the suffix construction expressing knowledge-based information turns into an evidential construction designating experiential information (cf. Section 3.5). Finally, the expansion from inference parameter to hearsay parameter in evidential -*rasi-i* is caused by an increase in conceptualizers and layering structures (cf. Section 3.3).

4.2. Previous research on *-rasi-i*

The Japanese evidential markers *-soo=da* and *-rasi-i* are categorized as designating 'judgement based on some evidence' (NKBK 2003). This definition fits with the one provided by Aikhenvald (2004), who defined grammatical evidentiality with reference to the 'source of information.' As I showed in Chapter 1, there are two ways in which *-rasi-i* is used: its suffixal usage and its evidential usage. The suffixal usage of *-rasi-i*, as exemplified by (1a), signifies 'a typical image of a person, things, or events, which people generally have' (Teramura 1984: 243). The evidential marker *-rasi-i* can express two different evidential parameters: inference or hearsay. The first, as shown in (1b), denotes the extrapolation of information through observation, while the second shown in (1c), denotes extrapolation based on information mentioned to the speaker by others.

(1) a. *Kare=wa totemo otoko-rasi-i.* [Typicality]
   3SG=TOP very man-AS-NPST.
   'He is a very real man.'
   b. *Tanaka=no heya=no dentoo=ga kie-te ir-u.*
   Tanaka=GEN room=GEN light=NOM turn off-GER be-NPST
   dooyara ne-te ir-u-rasi-i. [Inference]
   apparently sleep-GER be-NPST-INFR-NPST
   'Look at Tanaka's room. The light is out, so he must be in bed.'
   c. *Tizin=no hanasi=de=wa, ano mise=no keieisya=ga*
   acquaintance=GEN story=COP.INF=TOP DIST shop=GEN owner=NOM
   kawat-ta-rasi-i. [Hearsay]
   change-PST-HS-NPST
   'My friend told me that the owner of the shop had changed.'
   (NKBK 2003: 168–169)

The suffixal usage of *-rasi-i* combines with a noun to constitute an adjective.[1] The suffix *-rasi-i* can be tied to pronouns (2a), proper nouns (2b), and common nouns (2c) in the following ways:

(2) a. *Yuuzin-tati=wa kono watasi=no hatugen=o kii-te, ikanimo anata-rasi-i to warat-ta.*
   'My friends chuckled at my remarks and said, "It's so you."'
   b. *Kokizami=ni 7 ten=o ubat-ta. Izuremo honruida=de tatakidasi-ta at-ari-ga, ikanimo hakairyoku tappuri=no tyuuniti-rasi-i.*
   '(The baseball team "Tuuniti") scored 7 runs, each of which were scored through home runs. It's so typically Tuunichi, who have many sluggers'

c. *'Kaku=nara zizitu kankei=dake=de yoi'* to ii, *azikega-na-i* to *i-u* to *'azikenanka irana-i. Zizitu=dake=de yoi'* to *syutyoo-si-ta. Ikanimo kagakusya<u>-rasi-i</u>.*
'If I wrote a biography, I would write a record of facts' said Mr. Yamashina. When others said, "It's dull," he answered, "That's enough. Only the facts are required to be written in it." He's such a scientist.

(Miyake 2006: 129)

The suffixal usage of *-rasi-i* inflects in the same manner as other Japanese adjectives, unlike its evidential usage. As shown below, *-rasi-sa* is the substantivized form, *-rasi-ku* functions like an adverbial —— which is a modifier qualifying a predicate —— and *-rasi-ku-na-i* is the negative form of *-rasi-i*.[2]

(3) a. Substantivized form *-rasi-sa*
    e.g.) *Kare=no   otoko-rasi-sa=ni   odoroi-ta.*
         3SG=GEN   man-AS-NMLZ=DAT surprise-PST
    'I was surprised by his manhood.'
  b. Adverbial form to qualify a predicate *-rasi-ku*
    e.g.) *Kare=wa otoko-rasi-ku koodoo-si-ta.*
         3SG=TOP man-AS-ADV action-VS-PST
    'He acted like a man.'
  c. Negative form *-rasi-ku-na-i*
    e.g.) *Kare=wa hontoo=ni otoko-rasi-ku-na-i.*
         3SG=TOP real=DAT man-AS-VBLZ-NEG-NPST
    'He is really not masculine.'

As stated above, the evidential usage of *-rasi-i* can either denote inference or hearsay. The evidential usage of *-rasi-i* can be followed by ending particles, but not by the interrogative marker *-ka?* or the negative marker *-na-i*, as illustrated below:

(4) *Asita=wa   ame {-rasi-i=yo / -rasi-i=ne / *-rasi-i=ka?*
   tomorrow=TOP rain {-HS-NPST-SEP /-HS-NPST-SEP / *-EV-NPST-INT
   / *-rasi-ku-na-i}.
   / *-EV-VBLZ-NEG-NPST}
   'It'll rain tomorrow.'

The evidential usage can take the form 'noun + *-rasi-i.*' Although this may appear to be similar to the suffixal usage, it is interpreted as consisting of a nominal clause followed by the evidential marker *-rasi-i*.

(5) a. *Ano   hito=wa   nihonzin-rasi-i.* 'inferential evidential.'
       DIST   man=TOP   Japanese-INFR-NPST.
       'The man seems Japanese.'
    b. *Ano   hatugen=wa   nihonzin-rasi-i*
       DIST   statement=TOP   Japanese-AS-NPST
       hassoo=da.   'suffixal usage.'
       idea=COP.
       'The statement is a Japanese-like idea.'

(Asakawa and Takebe 2014: 320)

Both inference and hearsay follow a finite clause when expressed by the evidential usage of *-rasi-i*, but their constructional features differ. A sentence with the evidential *-rasi-i* after a conditional clause cannot be interpreted as an inference, being naturally understood to be hearsay instead.

(6) *Mosi   asita   ame=ga   hut-ta=ra,*
    If   tomorrow   rain=NOM   fall-PST=COND
    undookai=wa   tyuusi=ni   naru-rasi-i.   [*Inference/Hearsay]
    sports day=TOP   suspension=DAT   be-HS-NPST
    'If it rains tomorrow, the sports day will be called off.'

(7) *Taro=no   hanasi=de=wa,*   [*Mosi asita   ame=ga   hut-ta=ra,*
    Taro=GEN   story=COP.INF=TOP   [If tomorrow   rain=NOM   fall-PST=COND
    undookai=wa   tyuusi=ni   naru]   -rasi-i.   [Hearsay]
    sports day=TOP   suspension=DAT   be]   -HS-NPST
    'Taro told me, "If it rains tomorrow, the sports day will be called off."'

The inference designates extrapolation based on evidence the speaker has found, because the inferential *-rasi-i* cannot be used in such a hypothetical situation. It is unproblematic, however, if we interpret the sentence with the evidential marker *-rasi-i* after a conditional clause, as in Taro's statement in the sentence (7). Here the hearsay marker *-rasi-i* follows a complex sentence designating the information provided by Taro, namely that if it rains the next day, the sports day will be called off. The difference between the two parameters lies in the range of their syntactic scope, which determines the kind of structure preceding the evidential *-rasi-i*. That is to say, when used as a hearsay parameter, *-rasi-i* can follow either a simple sentence or a complex sentence, whereas when used as an inference parameter, it can follow only a simple sentence. The syntactic difference is deeply related to the difference in how the conceptualizer assesses the proposition designated by the sentence with the evidential *-rasi-i*. The inference parameter mainly refers to speakers' assessments based on evidence that they possess, since the propositions they state cannot be canceled by themselves. On the other hand, the hearsay parameter can be canceled by the speaker because the proposition designated by the sentence with the evidential *-rasi-i* is someone else's thought or information.

(8) a. ?? *Asioto=ga   sur-u.   Dareka=ga   heya=ni   hait-te*
        Footstep=NOM do-NPST someone-NOM room=DAT enter-GER
        ki-ta-rasi-i=ga,   watasi=wa soo omowa-na-i. [Inference]
        come-PST-INFR-NPST=ADVRS 1SG=TOP so think-NEG-NPST
        'I hear footsteps approaching. Someone may come into the room, but I don't think so.'
    b. *Sensei=no   hanasi=de=wa,   taro=wa   kaze=de*
        Teacher=GEN story=COP.INF=TOP Taro=TOP cold=CSL
        kesseki-rasi-i-ga,   watasi=wa soo omowa-na-i. [Hearsay]
        absence-HS-NPST=ADVRS 1SG=TOP so think-NEG-NPST
        'Our teacher said that Taro was absent because he got a cold, but I don't think so.'

4.2.1. The relationship between inference and hearsay: Kida (2013)

Kida (2013) argued that evidential *-rasi-i* has to a semantically unambiguous meaning, the polysemy (inference versus hearsay) being attributable to the type of reasoning used in the pragmatic process of interpreting the utterance. In particular, the difference between inference and hearsay arises not from the accessibility of the information, but from the inferential process of handling the information. The semantic meaning of the evidential *-rasi-i* provided by Kida (2013) is outlined below:

(9) the semantic meaning in the sentence 'P *-rasi-i*'
    'P *-rasi-i*' refers to 'P is the conclusion inferred from a given premise.'
                                                                    (Kida 2013: 98)

The two parameters were distinguished by testing for alternative paraphrasing. If *-rasi-i* refers to inference, it can be alternated with the evidential *-yoo=da* that designates inference. If *-rasi-i* denotes hearsay, it can be alternated with the evidential *-soo=da*, which expresses hearsay.

Although the difference between inference and hearsay had been assumed to be due to the accessibility of the information (i.e. directness vs. indirectness), Kida pointed out that this difference cannot be explained through the accessibility framework. If directly accessible information is defined as information that the speaker obtains directly, while indirectly accessible information is that which is based on what someone else told the speaker, then the inference parameter results from directly accessible information and the hearsay parameter arises from the indirectly accessible information. However, the accessibility-based definition falls short when the following case is considered. In sentence (10), Kida (2013) assumes a situation in which a critic of education has stated in the newspaper that the academic ability of university students is declining. He claimed that, in the spite of the fact that both sentences with *-rasi-i* in (10) were attributed to indirect accessible information (i.e. the critic's statement), they could be alternated with *-yoo=da*, which would mean that they designated the inference parameter.

(10) a. *Kono otoko=wa daigaku kyooiku=no zittai=o mattaku rikai-si-te i-na-i-rasi-i.*
 'The critic doesn't seem to grasp the real condition of the education at university at all.'
 b. *Saikin=no daigakusei=wa benkyoo=o si-na-ku-nat-ta-rasi-i.*
 'University students today seem to lose interest in studying.'

(Kida 2013: 100)

Given this discussion, Kida (2013: 101) insisted that the difference between inference and hearsay resulted from a different type of reasoning. The case of the evidential *-rasi-i* being interpreted as an inferential parameter was attributed to the type of reasoning shown below. The arrow describes the process of reasoning from a premise to a conclusion.

(11) a. hearing a noise → someone is there
 b. seeing people putting up umbrellas → it is raining outside.

This type of reasoning is called 'abductive reasoning,' which is the kind of reasoning wherein a cause is offered as the most rational explanation of a given phenomenon. The case of the evidential *-rasi-i* being interpreted as hearsay parameter was based on the following type of reasoning.

(12) a. X said 'the academic ability of university students was declining'.
 → I also conceive that the academic ability of university students is declining
 b. X said 'business was beginning to pick up next year'.
 → I also conceive that business is beginning to pick up next year

(Kida 2013: 101)

This type of reasoning is called 'reasoning from authority.' It evolved from the rhetorical 'argument from authority,' which is an argument in which the opinion of an authority is drawn on as evidence to support one's own argument. In this case, the 'authority' is the body of informants who are the source of information in the information flow.

His claim is a compelling explanation of how we can make two types of sentences with both parameters of evidential -*rasi-i* based on the common premise shown below. Considering that we can make these two sentences with -*rasi-i*, it makes no sense to attribute these different meanings to the accessibility of the information. Thus, it is a reasonable explanation that they result from different types of reasoning.

(13) The common premise: an educational critic stated that the academic ability of university students was declining.
 →(reasoning from authority) The academic ability of university students was declining.
 →(abductive reasoning) The critic doesn't seem to grasp the real condition of the education at university at all.
(Kida 2013: 103)

4.2.2. The relationship between suffixal and evidential -*rasi-i*: Miyake (2006)

Miyake (2006) presented a comprehensive analysis of the relationship between the suffixal and evidential usages of -*rasi-i* by employing two cognitive linguistic frameworks: 'an approach based on schema' and 'an approach based on prototype.' They are outlined below:

(14) a. An approach based on schema
 The essential meaning, called 'schema,' is abstracted from all of the usages, which are instantiated from the schema.
 b. An approach based on prototype
 Assume the most primary usage to be the 'prototype' for all of the usages and that the other usages are extended from the prototypical usage.
(Miyake 2006: 124–125)

Miyake (2006) considered the suffix -*rasi-i* to designate "typical feature" and the evidential to denote 'empirically based assessment.'[3] He claimed that the evidential usage is semantically extended from the suffixal usage, both of which are instantiated from the schema 'contiguity.' The meaning 'typical feature' expressed by the suffixal usage is a usage to describe 'the typical feature of the noun followed by *-rasi-i*' (Miyake 2006: 129). In sentence (15), the adjectival phrase *anata-rasi-i* 'very you' refers to the prototypical feature of the referent designated by the noun *anata* 'you'. On the other hand, the evidential usage signifies an empirical assessment (i.e. inferential parameter). As exemplified by (16), a sentence with *-rasi-i* expresses an extrapolation attributed to perceiving the situation (e.g. seeing men sucking candies) as evidence.

(15)(=2a)
 Yuuzintati=wa kono watasi=no hatugen=o kii-te, ikanimo anata-rasi-i to warat-ta.
 'My friends chuckled at my remarks and said, "It's so you."'

(Miyake 2006: 129)

(16) *Asa=no densya=no naka=de, amedama=o syabur-u otokotati=ga hue-te ir-u-no=da. Hirusugi=no gaitoo=demo, arui=wa yoru=no takusii=no naka=demo, ame=o name-te iru hito+bito=ga ir-u. Dooyara ame=ga oohayari=no yononaka-rasi-i.*
 'I see more men sucking candies on the trains in the mornings. Even on the streets in the early afternoon or in a taxi at night, I see men sucking candies. Apparently, candies are booming in this world.'

(Miyake 2006: 121)

As regards the schema, in the case of the suffixal usage meaning 'typical feature,' the referent designated by the noun in the adjectival phrase '[noun] *-rasi-i*' has a contiguous relationship with the referent's prototypical feature (e.g. *kodomo-rasi-i* 'childlike': the relationship between the noun *kodomo* 'child' and its prototypical feature 'innocence/crying all the time'). In the construction '[proposition] *-rasi-i*' that describes an empirical assessment, the schema 'contiguity' is reflected in the way in which the process of finding evidence is connected to the proposition. The two usages are continuous categories because, as shown in (17), the phrase *sinzin-rasi-i* is an ambiguous expression (i.e. 'the nurse is newcomer-like' versus, 'the nurse seems like a newcomer.'), which means that this sentence is a link between the suffixal usage and the evidential usage.

(17) *Kaeri giwa, sinzin-rasi-i kangosi=ga issyookenmei soozi=o si-te i-masi-ta.*
 'When I left there, {the newcomer-like nurse / the nurse seeming a newcomer} was cleaning up vigorously.'

(Miyake 2006: 131)

Finally, Miyake (2006) stated that the hearsay parameter of -*rasi-i* is the same as the empirical assessment in the sense that it has evidence for conceiving the proposition as true, but the process of finding evidence is much shorter than for the one designated by the inference parameter (Miyake 2006: 123). In sum, Miyake (2006) tried to explain the two usages of -*rasi-i* holistically by setting up the schema 'contiguity.' He claimed that it was possible that the suffixal usage was connected to the evidential usage as a holistic continuous category.

4.2.3. What is at issue?

I take the same position as Miyake (2006) in that I advocate for the holistic approach to the usages of -*rasi-i*. However, I believe that in order to accurately describe its different usages in a holistic way, it is necessary to consider the language change of -*rasi-i*. Two issues deserve attention in our discussion of language change. First, though evidential -*rasi-i* was developed from its suffixal usage, the process of this language change requires further exploration. As stated above, the suffixal usage inflects in the same way as Japanese adjectives as shown in (18), but evidential -*rasi-i* does not have such inflectional forms.

(18)(=3)
    a. Substantivized form -*rasi-sa*
        e.g.) *Kare=no otoko-rasi-sa=ni   odoroi-ta.*
            3SG=GEN man-AS-NMLZ=DAT surprise-PST
        'I was surprised by his manhood.'
    b. Adverbial form qualifying a predicate -*rasi-ku*
        e.g.) *Kare=wa otoko-rasi-ku   koodoo-si-ta.*
            3SG=TOP man-AS-ADV   action-VS-PST
        'He acted like a man.'
    c. Negative form -*rasi-ku-na-i*
        e.g.) *Kare=wa hontoo=ni otoko-rasi-ku-na-i.*
            3SG-TOP   real=DAT   man-AS-ADV-NEG-NPST
        'He is really not masculine.'

(19) a. *Dooyara, hayame=ni syuppatu-suru {-rasi-i   / *-rasi-sa*
      apparently early=DAT departure-VS {-INFR-NPST / *-INFR-NMLZ
      / **-rasi-ku-na-i}.*
      / *-INFR-ADV-NEG-NPST}
      'Apparently, they are going to leave early.'
    b. *Tanaka=ni   yoru=to,   Katoo=wa   raisyuu*
      Tanaka=DAT   accord=COND Kato=TOP   next week
      hikkos-u   {-rasi-i / *-rasi-sa / *-rasi-ku-na-i}.

move home-NPST {-HS-NPST / *-HS-NMLZ/ *-HS-ADV-NEG-NPST}
'According to Tanaka, Kato will move home next week.'

To manifest the entire language change of -*rasi-i*, we have to describe it not only from the aspect of its semantic change but also in terms of its constructional change from the suffixal construction [[noun] -*rasi-i*] to the evidential construction [[proposition] -*rasi-i*].

Secondly, the relationship between the inference parameter and the hearsay parameter designated by -*rasi-i* has to be reconsidered from the perspective of language change. Miyake (2006) explained the difference between inference parameter and hearsay as the length of a search process to connect evidence with a proposition. He insisted that the search process in the hearsay parameter is much shorter than the one designated by the inference parameter. However, the search process was not well defined, leaving the explanation of the difference still unclear. From my perspective, it seems that the hearsay parameter requires a longer distance and search process between the proposition and the evidence, first because it requires an additional participant, one who has given information to the speaker, and second because, in a situation where the speaker has received information from that participant, the speaker must reconstruct what the participant said. Although Kida (2013) pointed out that the difference between them was due to a difference in pragmatic reasoning, this assumption that the two parameters are determined by different pragmatical processes of reasoning (i.e. 'abductive reasoning' versus 'reasoning from authority') loses sight of the following difference in semantic-syntactic scope between the two parameters.

(20)(=6)
Mosi   asita   ame=ga   hut-ta=ra,   undookai=wa
If   tomorrow   rain=NOM   fall-PST=COND   sports day=TOP
tyuusi=ni   naru-rasi-i.   [*Inference / Hearsay]
suspension=DAT   be-EV-NPST
'If it rains tomorrow, the sports day will be called off.'

(21)(=7)
Taro=no   hanasi=de=wa,   [Mosi   asita   ame=ga
Taro=GEN   story=COP.INF=TOP [If   tomorrow rain=NOM
hut-ta=ra,   undookai=wa   tyuusi=ni   naru]   -rasi-i.   [Hearsay]
fall-PST=COND sports day=TOP suspension=DAT be] -HS-NPST
'Taro told me, "If it rains tomorrow, the sports day will be called off."'

As stated above, the sentence with evidential -*rasi-i* after a conditional clause cannot be interpreted as an inference, being naturally understood instead as hearsay. The inference parameter designated by *-rasi-i* has to be an extrapolation based on some evidence discovered by the speaker. Therefore *-rasi-i* cannot be used as an inference parameter in a hypothetical situation. However, if evidential *-rasi-i* issued as a hearsay parameter (e.g. Taro's statement in (21)), the sentence is acceptable because the semantic-syntagmatic scope of *-rasi-i* covers the complex sentence that designates the information that others conveyed to the speaker. As part of this discussion, it is necessary to focus on the fact that this difference in scope is deeply related to the difference in the identity of the conceptualizer assessing the proposition designated by the sentence with evidential *-rasi-i*. While the inference parameter refers to the speaker's assessment based on their own evidence, the hearsay parameter designates someone else's thoughts or information. Thus, propositions based on inference cannot be canceled by the speakers themselves, while those based on hearsay can be.

(22)(=8)
   a. ??*Asioto=ga   sur-u.   Dareka=ga   heya=ni   hait-te*
        Footstep=NOM   do-NPST.   Someone=NOM   room=DAT   enter-GER
        ki-ta-rasi-i=ga,   watasi=wa   soo   omowa-na-i. [Inference]
        come-PST-INFR-NPST=ADVRS   1SG=TOP   so   think-NEG-NPST.
        'I hear footsteps approaching. Someone may come into the room, but I don't think so.'
   b. *Sensei=no   hanasi=de=wa,   taro=wa   kaze=de*
        Teacher=GEN   story=COP.INF=TOP   Taro=TOP   cold=CSL
        kesseki-rasi-i=ga,   watasi=wa   so   omowa-na-i. [Hearsay]
        absent-HS-NPST=ADVRS   1SG=TOP   so   think-NEG-NPST
        'Our teacher said that Taro was absent because he got a cold, but I don't think so.'

From the perspective of CG theory, this difference is caused by a change in the part preceding *-rasi-i* from process to proposition (cf. Figure 3.7). This means that the development of *-rasi-i* is associated with a constructional change. Given these facts, it is obvious that the difference between the inferential parameter and hearsay parameter of *-rasi-i* is related to constructional factors. Thus, it is more than merely a pragmatic difference such as one in inferential process.

    The language change of *-rasi-i* is marked by an expansion of its semantic-syntactic scope, namely the element preceding *-rasi-i* changes from a noun to a finite clause. Along with this change, suffixal *-rasi-i* is grammaticalized to become evidential *-rasi-i*. The expanded scope is also related to the rise of the hearsay parameter of *-rasi-i*. In this chapter, in order to elucidate the constructional and semantic changes of *-rasi-i*, I will overview the framework of grammaticalization and incorporate the 'expansion model' of grammaticalization proposed by Traugott (2010b).

4.3. Grammaticalization

Grammaticalization is a process of language change, as defined below:

(23) Grammaticalization is defined as the development from lexical to grammatical forms, and from grammatical to even more grammatical forms.

(Heine and Kuteva 2007: 32)

Heine and Kuteva (2007) stated there are two kinds of criteria for describing grammaticalization. The first is diachronic criteria. Grammaticalization theory is based on generalizations of historical process, therefore 'its hypotheses must be verifiable, or falsifiable, by means of historical data' (Heine and Kuteva 2007: 212). The other is structural criteria. 'Since grammaticalization is a regular process, instances of it can also be identified by means of structural properties' (Heine and Kuteva 2007: 213). The structural properties differ between grammatical expressions and non-grammatical ones with reference to the following four parameters:

(24) Parameters of grammaticalization
    a. extension, i.e. the rise of new grammatical meaning when linguistic expressions are extended to new contexts (context-induced reinterpretation)
    b. desemanticization (or "semantic bleaching"), i.e. loss (or generalization) in meaning content.
    c. decategorialization, i.e. loss in the morphosyntactic properties characteristic of lexical or other less grammaticalized forms.
    d. erosion ("phonetic reduction"), i.e. loss in phonetic substance.

(Heine and Kuteva 2007: 34)

Extension is the process in which a novel grammatical meaning arises when an expression is extended to contexts where the expression has never been used before, therefore it focuses on the pragmatic aspect of language changes. Heine and Kuteva (2007) presented the process of extension as the following four-stage model:

Table 4.1. The model of extension (context-induced reinterpretation)

Stage	Context	Resulting meaning	Type of inference
I Initial stage	Unconstrained	Source meaning	—
II Bridging context	There is a new context triggering a new meaning.	Target meaning foregrounded	Invited (cancellable)
III Switch context	There is a new context which is incompatible with the source meaning.	Source meaning backgrounded	Usual (typically no-cancellable)
IV Conventionalization	The target meaning no longer needs to be supported by the context that gave rise to it; it may be used in new contexts.	Target meaning only	—

(Heine and Kuteva 2007: 37)

This model shows the transition from less grammatical meaning in Stage I to more grammatical meaning in Stage IV. The more grammatical meaning does not arise directly from Stage I, but only through transitional second and third stages. In the intermediate stages, the new context first triggers a new meaning and then backgrounds the existing meaning, the two processes being related to the two possible factors of 'semantic generalization' and 'invited inferencing' respectively. The author utilized the transition of the English preposition *in* as an example.

(25) a. John died in London.
b. John died in Iraq.
c. John died in a car accident.

(Heine and Kuteva 2007: 37)

Semantic generalization is interchangeable with semantic bleaching, wherein 'new contexts entail a more general meaning' (Heine and Kuteva 2007: 36). In (25a), the term *in* functions as a special preposition, with a similar function applying to sentence (25b). When the preposition *in* is extended to sentence (25c), however, the meaning is no longer limited to the spatial realm and becomes a more general one that applies to wider contexts. That is, in the words of Heine and Kuteva (2007:36), 'the more contexts of use a linguistic expression acquires, the more it tends to lose in semantic specificity and to undergo semantic generalization.' Concomitantly, when an expression is used in a specific context where it has never been used before, the new context can trigger new meanings that arise from invited inference. Although the preposition *in* in (25a) designates only spatial meaning, as it is extended to (25b), encyclopedic knowledge triggers an invited inference to associate an event with a place, such as a war-torn location. The causal event meaning (*John died in Iraq* (war)) arises from the spatial meaning (*John died in Iraq* (place)) via the invited inference. In sentence (25b), since the spatial meaning could also be appropriate depending on the context, the causal event meaning generated by the invited inference can be cancelable (e.g. *John died in Iraq, the place not the war.*). However, in sentence (25c), the spatial meaning is backgrounded, and the only reasonable meaning of *in* is the causal event. In this stage, the meaning 'causal event' is entrenched in one of the usages of the preposition *in*.

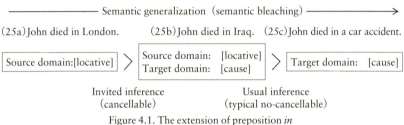

Figure 4.1. The extension of preposition *in*

Desemanticization, which is related to the aspect of semantics, refers to the phenomenon wherein a language expression loses a part of its meaning and acquires a new meaning when it is extended to a new context. Desemanticization results from the semantic generalization of the extension. For example, body part terms can be reinterpreted as locative adpositions (e.g. back > behind, head > on top of) and action verbs as tense and aspectual markers (e.g. keep > keep -ing, go to > be going to). In contexts where these language expressions are extended, these concrete meanings (body part or physical movement) are bleached out, consequently giving way to more schematic meanings (spatial meaning or temporal, aspectual relations).

As Heine and Kuteva (2007: 40) stated, 'Once a linguistic expression has been desemanticized, for example from a lexical to a grammatical meaning, it tends to lose morphological and syntactic properties characterizing its earlier use but being no longer relevant to its new use.' These morphological and syntactic changes, called 'decategorialization,' have the following salient properties:

(26) Salient properties of decategorialization
   a. Loss of ability to be inflected.
   b. Loss of ability to take on derivational morphology.
   c. Loss of ability to take modifiers.
   d. Loss of independence as an autonomous form, increasing dependence

on some other form.
e. Loss of syntactic freedom, e.g. of the ability to be moved around in the sentence in ways that are characteristic of the non-grammaticalized source item.
f. Loss of ability to be referred to anaphorically.
g. Loss of members belonging to the same grammatical paradigm.

(Heine and Kuteva 2007: 40–41)

The gerundival or participle form (-*ing*) turns into one that serves propositional function (e.g. barring, concerning, considering). Additionally, verbs lose most of their verbal properties, no longer being inflected for tense or aspect, for example, and unable to take auxiliaries. The verb *consider* in sentence (27a) retains its verbal properties, such as the ability to be modified by an adverb (*carefully*), distinguishing between present or past (*considering* vs. *having considered*), taking the same subject in the main clause. In sentence (27b), on the other hand, where *considering* serves a purely conjunctional function, these verbal properties are not allowed.

(27) a. Carefully considering / Having carefully considered all the evidence, the panel delivered its verdict.
b. Considering (*Having carefully considered) you are so short, your skill at basketball is unexpected.

(Hopper and Traugott 2003: 127)

Decategorialization is not limited to the grammaticalizing process from a lexical to a grammatical item, but also applies to derivation from a less grammatical to a more grammatical item. As an example, the English clause subordinator *that* was derived from the demonstrative use of the word. Like other nouns and pronouns, demonstrative *that* is inflected for number, having *those* as its plural form. In its grammaticalized form as a clause subordinator, however, it is not inflected for number (e.g. *the books {that / *those } I know*). Therefore, the clause subordinator is a more grammatical form than the demonstrative, having lost the morphological status of noun and pronoun. Finally, 'erosion' is a phonetic process whereby a language expression loses its phonetic substance through grammaticalization. The phonetic transition of the conjunction *because* into *cuz* serves as a typical example of this process.

4.3.1. Unidirectionality: grammaticalization as reduction and expansion

Traugott (2010b) suggested the possibility that grammaticalization has two modes, which he termed the reduction model and the expansion model, as shown below:

(28) In the past thirty years two major approaches to grammaticalization have developed, which depend to a large extent on how 'grammar,' and especially morphosyntax, is conceptualized. One focuses on reduction and increased dependency, the other on expansion of various kinds. Both understand grammaticalization as a subset of possible language changes.

(Traugott 2010b: 269)

While the traditional grammaticalization known as reduction focused on morpho-syntactic change, the newer grammaticalization as expansion focuses on the functional, semantic and pragmatic factors involved in such change. Common to both grammaticalization is the emergence of a novel grammatical expression, the fundamental difference between them being whether the process of the emergence of the novel grammatical expression is accompanied by a reduction or an expansion in syntactic independency and scope[4].

Many scholars have pointed out that traditional grammaticalization is a unidirectional process involved not only in decategorialization and semantic generalization, both of which were overviewed in the previous chapter, but also in reducing the scope and reducing syntactic independency, which means that the grammaticalized item becomes morphologically dependent on another lexical item. This traditional grammaticalization has been called the 'reduction model' (Traugott 2010b). In this model, the transition from a content word or a less grammatical word to a more grammatical word is considered to be a process of transforming independent items into dependent ones. In other words, an expression loses its morpho-syntactic independence, becoming dependent on another constituent in the sentence. Brinton and Traugott (2005) highlighted the following three levels of fusion with external elements.

(29) G1 = periphrases, e.g. *be going to, as far as, in fact* (in their early stages),
G2 = semi-bound forms like function words and clitics, e.g. *must, of, -'ll*, genitive *—s* (many function words are cliticized in some positions, but free in others, e.g., *of*, which can be stranded as in *That's all I can think of*),
G3 = affixes such as derivational morphology that changes the grammatical class of the stem, e.g., adverbial *-wise* (fairly productive); most especially inflectional morphology (very productive; sometimes default), including zero inflection (Bybee 1994).

(Brinton and Traugott 2005: 93)

The varying levels of the stages show the degree of grammaticity, which increases from the periphrase level of G1 to the affixal level of G3. The direction of grammaticity only goes forward to a more grammatical stage, never backward. In summary, the reduction model of grammaticalization focuses on the morpho-syntactic features, whose development (e.g. periphrases > function words and clitic > affix) has been regarded as the main factor in grammaticalization.

In contrast to the reduction model of grammaticalization, other scholars, while maintaining the categories of decategorialization and semantic generalization, have highlighted the language changes involved in the expansion of syntactic independency and scope. Some examples are provided below:

(30) a. as long as: as long as [NP] > as long as [Clause]
     b. a sort of: a sort of [NP] > a sort of [XP] > a sort of [Clause]

As indicated in (30a), a construction with a nominal phrase within the scope of *as long as* developed into a construction in which a finite clause has been taken into the scope. Thus, the conjunction *as long as* was grammaticalized from its prepositional usage (e.g. *This plank is as long as that one.* > *Hold it in place as long as it is needed.*). Similar to the grammaticalization of *as long as*, the discourse marker *sort of* was developed due to an expansion of its scope (e.g. *a sort of [apple]* > *He's sort of [weird]* > *[I am a queen], sort of.*) (cf. Hayase 2014: 22). Likewise, discourse markers *indeed* and *in fact* were grammaticalized through the path [verbal adverb > sentence adverb > discourse marker] once those elements took an expanded constituent into their scope. In addition, *sort of* can be used independently in a conversation to offer an ambiguous response, as illustrated below:

(31) A: What happened to you? Are you Okay?
     B: Sort of (sorta).

This indicates that the discourse marker is highly independent of any syntactic relationship. This type of grammaticalization involved in the expansion of syntactic independency and its scope is called the 'expansion model' (Traugott 2010b).

In Japanese language change, the development of a function word due to decreased dependency, which was highlighted by Koyanagi (2013a), is thought to be an example of the expansion model. Based on different sources, Koyanagi (2013a) indicated that there are four types of productive processes through which Japanese grammatical items are developed.[5]

Table 4.2. The process of producing function words

	From one source	From multiple source
Content word	Development to function word (Increased dependency)	
Functional word	Multi-functionalization	Compounding functional words
Affix	Development to functional word (decreased dependency)	

(Koyanagi 2013a: 69)

Functionalization is a language change in which a grammatical word acquires another grammatical function. Functionalization has two types of development. The first is multi-functionalization, which is caused by an extension of the meanings of a function word. The nominative case marker =*ga* acquired an additional conjunctive usage as one of its meanings. The other way is to compound function words to create a new function word. As shown in (33), the particle -*baya*, which designates optative mood, is a compound word consisting of the subjunctive particle =*ba* and the interrogative =*ya*.

(32) -*ga*:case marker (nominative)) → conjunction particle

(Koyanagi 2013a: 65)

(33) =*ba* (subjunctive) + =*ya* (interrogative particle) → =*baya* (optative mood)

(Koyanagi 2013a: 69)

Key to understanding the development of function words is the concept of syntactic dependency. As generally defined, grammatical elements inevitably depend on the lexical element in a sentence. Thus, affixes exhibit greater syntactic dependency and content words less syntactic dependency, with function words occupying an intermediate position between the two. Function words can therefore develop in either of two ways: through the increasing dependency of a lexical item or through the decreasing dependency of an affix. This is illustrated in the following table.

Table 4.3. The two methods of function word development

Content words	>	Function words	<	Affix
	Development to functional word (Increasing dependency)		Development to functional word (Decreasing dependency)	

Based on this scale, Koyanagi (2013a) propounded two types of function word development: one based on increasing dependency and the other on decreasing dependency. The Japanese particle *-take* in (34) is an example of development based on increasing dependency, where the function word *-take* that serves as a particle was developed from the noun *take*, meaning 'the length or height of things,' by fusing other lexical elements. Since the function word was grammaticalized due to an increase in its dependency on other lexical items in the sentence, it could be said that this development falls under the reduction model.

(34) *Take* (noun)
→ *ari=take tuka-u* (quantity) → *niger-u=dake niger-u* (degree) → *doug-u=-dake=wa ar-u* (only thing)

The mood particle *-mu* in old Japanese, as shown in (35), was grammaticalized from the suffix *-mu* converting an adjective form into a verb form. The suffix designated the change of state expressed by the adjective that followed, as exemplified by (36). After that, the suffix acquired the meaning 'prediction for a change of state,' and was eventually extended in meaning to become a function word expressing grammatical mood referring to unrealized event.

(35) *ita-mu* (verbal suffix) → *saka-mu* 'it will bloom' (a functional word referring to an irreal event as a mood)

(Koyanagi 2013a: 68)

(36) a. *itasi* >   *ita-mu*   (get pain, feel pain)
     b. *suzusi* > *suzu-mu* (get cool, cool down)
     c. *usi* >   *u-mu*   (get fed up)

(Koyanagi 2013a: 254)

(37) *Yuusa=reba Sio mitinaku-**mu** Suminoe=no Asaka=no ura=ni Tamamo karitena*
'When evening falls, the salt tide will come flooding in, and that is when I would go down to Suminoe to gather gem weed in Asaka Bay.'

(*Manyosyu*, Vol.2, No. 121: Translated by Cranston (1998))

Assuming Koyanagi (2013a) is correct in his analysis of the language change involved here, in this case the constituent followed by *-mu* shifted from an adjectival stem to a verb itself, which means that its dependency on other lexical items decreased, for the development of the Japanese term *-mu* coincided with the expansion model of grammaticalization. Koyanagi (2013a) also pointed out that the function word development model that involved a decrease in dependency was found in old Japanese because grammatical meaning in old Japanese was represented by many affixal elements, which meant that word-formation based on those affixes was extremely productive.

4.4. The emergence of Japanese evidentialities

Tracing the historical transition of evidential -*rasi-i* in Japanese reveals that it was derived from the suffixal usage of the term -*rasi-i*. This kind of path is not just limited to -*rasi-i*. Interestingly enough, other Japanese evidentials also followed a similar path. These include the evidentials -*gena*, which initially represented inference and hearsay parameters, and -*soo=da*, which presently denotes the hearsay parameter. Both were derived from a suffix which acquired evidential meaning as a function word, a process which took place before the evidential usage of -*rasi-i* was established. In this chapter, I will overview the emergence of evidential markers in Japanese. The historical division of Japanese is laid out in Table 4.4. This is the traditional five-way classification, which I will follow in this chapter.

Table 4.4. The historical division of Japanese

Binary	Five-way	Period / Century
Ancient Japanese	Old	~ Nara Period: the 6th ~ the late 8th century
	Early Middle	Heian Period: the late 8th century ~ the late 11th century
	Late Middle	Kamakura Period ~ Muromachi Period: the late 11th century ~ the late 17th century
Modern Japanese	Early Modern	Edo Period: the early 17th century ~ the middle of 19th century
	Modern	Post Meiji Period: 1868 ~

4.4.1. The historical transition of -*gena* and -*sauna* (-*soo=da*): Senba (1972)

Senba (1972) focused on the historical transition of the Japanese evidentials -*gena* and -*soo=da*, both of which developed from suffixal usages and then acquired the evidential meaning of hearsay after they were extended from inferential evidential markers. Senba (1972) summarized the historical transition as follows:

(38) -*gena*

Evidential -*gena*, which follows the finite clause,[6] originally referred to an inference parameter. It acquired the hearsay parameter during the Muromachi Period and was mainly used as a hearsay parameter in Early Modern Period.

(39) -*sau=na* (-*soo=da*)[7]
    i) In the late Muromachi Period, the evidential -*sau=na* emerged, originally being used as an inference parameter.
    ii) In the middle of the Edo Period, the evidential -*sau=na* acquired its usage as a hearsay parameter. The frequency of -*sau=na* as a hearsay parameter gradually increased. Its usage then eventually became limited to hearsay. In other words, its inference parameter was desemanticized during the Meiji Period.

The evidential -*gena* was originally derived from the nominal adjectival suffix -*genar-i*. The suffix -*genar-i* was used for describing appearance, as shown below:

(40) *To, ikimo taetutu, kikoe mahos-i-genar-u koto=wa ari-gena=redo, ito **kurus-i-geni** tayu-gena=reba,* [...]
    'Thus with faint voice and failing breath she whispered. But though she had found strength to speak, each word was uttered with great toil and pain.'
                    ('Kiritubo.' *The Tales of Genji*: Translated by Waley and Washburn, emphasis is mine)

From the Kamakura Period to the late Muromachi Period, the suffix -*genar-i* was used in a construction where it followed a finite clause form.[8] At the beginning, the construction expressed only the inference parameter, as shown below:

(41) [...] *Miuti=no zosiki hutari=mo 'Nanigoto=mo ara=ba issyo=ni-te=sooroo' to moosi=sooroo aida, **todomar-u-geni**=sooroo.*
    '[...] the political officers with him said that they would be with him anytime, so they seem to stay here.'
                                      (*Gikeiki*, emphasis is mine)

During the Edo Period, the evidential -*gena* began to represent the hearsay parameter. We can understand that -*gena* in sentence (42) obviously designates the hearsay parameter due to the phrase '*kike=ba* (from what I've gathered).'

(42) *Kike=ba, Yozibee-me=wa notare **sisi-ta-gena**.*

'I hear that Yojibee died like a dog.'

('Yamazaki Yojibee Nebiki no Kadomatu' *Tikamatu Jyoorurisyuu Jyo*, emphasis is mine)

The transition of the evidential *-gena* is summarized in Table 4.5. The origin of *-gena* is the nominal adjectival suffix *-genar-i*. The construction [[finite clause]-*gena*] that designates the inference parameter arose during the Kamakura Period and the late Muromachi Period. After that, the construction [[finite clause]-*gena*] acquired and entrenched the hearsay parameter. Concomitantly, the inferential usage decreased significantly. In modern Japanese grammar, though the suffix *-genar-i* is used for constructing a few lexical items (e.g. *ayasi-gena* (dubious), *imiari-gena* (sly)), it has a significantly lower productivity than other suffixes. The evidential usage of *-gena* is not established in modern standard Japanese grammar, but even now it is used in Western Japan and in the Kyuusyuu-dialect.[9]

Table 4.5. The language change of the evidential marker *-gena*

	Late Middle		Early Modern	Modern
	Heian-Kamakura Period	Muromachi Period		
Suffix	*-genar-i*	→	→	lexical item
Evidential (INFR)	[[finite clause]-*gena*]	→	(loss)	
Evidential (HS)		[[finite clause]-*gena*]	→	(dialect)

The modern Japanese evidential *-soo=da* has its origin in a suffixal usage, *-sauna*, which arose during the Muromachi Period. During the period ranging from the late Muromachi Period until the Edo Period, the suffix *-sauna*, which changed verbs and adjectives into nominal adjectives, developed into the evidential *-sau=na* that follows a finite clause. As is the case with the historical transition of *-gena*, the evidential *-sau=na* originally denoted the inference parameter.

(43) *Mesi=ni hi=ga hait-ta-sau=na. Koge kusa-i-wai=noo.*
'Someone has cooked rice. I smell it get burned.'

('Osanago Katakiuti' *Kabuki Kyakuhonsyuu Jyo*)

(Senba 1972: 524, emphasis is mine)

In the Edo Period, the evidential *-sau=na* began to denote the hearsay parameter, as shown in (44), where the owner tells his servant that his customer said that their companions would be coming there later.

(44) **Oture=mo ar-u-sou=na.** *Kireina zasiki=e toosi=masi=ya.*
   'He said his companions would be coming later. Could you show him into the beautiful parlor?'

   ('Aneimoto Dateno Okido' *Kyakuhonsyuu Ge*)
   (Senba 1972: 526, emphasis is mine)

During the Edo Period, -*sau=na* denoted the inference and hearsay parameters when it followed a finite clause. However, from then on, its inferential usage gradually decreased until it almost entirely disappeared during the Meiji Period.[10]

Table 4.6 summarizes the historical development of the evidential -*soo=da*, the modern evidential -*soo=da* that derived from the original suffix -*sau=na*, which first appeared in the Muromachi Period. Initially, -*soo=da* was limited to the inference parameter, and then the evidential -*sauna* acquired the hearsay parameter in the Edo Period. During this period, though the evidential -*soo=da* denoted both these two parameters, its inference parameter gradually fell into disuse. Ultimately, -*soo=da* was established as the evidential marker that denotes the hearsay parameter in modern Japanese.

Table 4.6. The language change of -*soo=da*

	Late Middle (Muromachi Period)	Early Modern (Edo Period)	Modern
Suffix	-*sauna* ──→		
Evidential (INFR)	[[finite clause]-*soo=da*]	──────────────→ (loss)	
Evidential (HS)		[[finite clause]-*soo=da*] ───→	

As is obvious from Tables 4.5 and 4.6, though he evidential -*gena* had been derived prior to the development of the evidential -*soo=da*, the two types of evidential markers followed the same historical developmental path. As regards the structural changes, the evidentials were derived from the suffixal usages. These evidentials had originally been limited in meaning to the inference parameter, but they gradually acquired the additional meaning of the hearsay parameter. After a while, the inference parameter of both these evidentials fell into disuse. Eventually, they were established in modern Japanese grammar as evidential markers.

Bybee et al. (1994) pointed out that grammaticalization has highly constrained and specifiable grammaticalization paths that lead to new grammatical constructions. The Japanese evidential modalities -*gena* and -*soo=da* have followed the language change presented below:

Table 4.7. The language change of evidentiality in Japanese

Part of Speech	Nominal adjective	>	Functional word (Evidential: INFR / HS)
Construction	[[Stem]-Suffix]	>	[[Finite clause]-EV]

In addition to the structural changes, it can be said that their meaning followed the same path because the evidential originally denoted the inference parameter and then acquired the meaning of hearsay evidential as well. From then on, in addition to the decreasing frequency of the inference parameter, the evidential specialized in representing the hearsay parameter.

4.4.2. The historical transition of -rasi-i

The modern Japanese evidential -rasi-i is derived from a suffixal usage that was used for forming adjectives. While the suffix -rasi-i follows a noun or the stem of a nominal adjective, the evidential -rasi-i follows a finite verb. In this respect, the evidential -rasi-i has taken the same path as the evidentials -gena and -soo=da, which were overviewed in the previous chapter. From a historical point of view, though the suffix -rasi-i first appeared in the Muromachi Period, the development of its evidential form occurred more recently than -gena and -soo=da since the frequency of its usage increased in the Meiji Period.[11]

4.4.2.1. The Late Middle Era (12c–16c)

The first appearance of the suffix -rasi-i was in the Late Middle Era (cf. Murakami 1981, Yamamoto 2012). The *Arte da Lingoa de Iapam* (Nihon Daibunten), edited by João Rodrigues in the Late Middle Era, contains information about the suffix -rasi-i. It states that the suffix -rasi-i denoted the typicality of or similarity with the noun that was followed by -rasi-i. In this era, some examples cannot be analyzed as [[noun] + suffix -rasi-i]. Those examples should be treated as a whole word. Although further study is required to determine whether or not these examples are related to the modern suffix -rasi-i, there is no problem with us connecting examples analyzed as [[noun] + suffix -rasi-i] to the modern suffix -rasi-i (e.g. *otoko-rasi-i* (a very man)). The following examples of the suffix -rasi-i are listed in the *Vocabulário da Língua do Japão* (Nippo Jisyo) from the late middle era (cf. Iwasaki 2013).

(45) *Vocabulário da Língua do Japão* (Nippo Jisyo)
    a. Xŏneraxij.   '*Syoone-rasi-i* (well-advised)'
       e.g.) Xŏneraxij fito. '*Syoone-rasi-i hito* (a person with good sense)'
    b. Vonagoraxij.   '*onago-rasi-i* (feminine)'

e.g.) Vonagoraxij fito. '*onagorasi-i hito* (a feminine woman or a feminine man)'
c. Votocoraxij.   '*otoko-rasi-i* (masculine, manful)'
e.g.) Votocoraxij vonna. (*otoko-rasi-i onna* 'a masculine woman')
d. Xucqeraxij.   '*syukke-rasi-i* (like a priest)'
e. Zocuraxij.   '*zoku-rasi-i* (like a secular)'

Although the suffix *-rasi-i* in modern Japanese follows pronouns and proper nouns as in *kare-rasi-i huruma-i* 'behavior entirely characteristic of him' and *Tanaka-rasi-i koodoo* 'behavior entirely characteristic of Tanaka,' the suffix was not so used in the Late Middle Era. This means that the adjective construction with the suffix *-rasi-i* at that time had little productivity and was used without chunking it, because it is reasonable to consider that the construction with the suffix *-rasi-i* functioned as the adjective construction [X-*rasi-i*].

4.4.2.2. The Early Modern Era (17c–18c)

At the dawn of the early modern era, new types of meanings and stems that were followed by *-rasi-i* emerged (cf. Yamamoto 2012: 172). First, the scope of *-rasi-i* expanded to cover not only a single noun but also nominal phrases like the construction [[X-no Y]-*rasi-i*], as shown below:

(46) *Mata tosi sanzyu-bakari-naru [gohukuya=no tedai]-rasi-ki=ga,* [...].
'And a man in his thirties who looks like a sales clerk of a draper, [...]'
('Jikyubanasi' *Hanasibon Taikei*, bracket is mine)

In addition, though the adjective construction [X-*rasi-i*] had originally been used to form an adjective meaning 'characterized by the typical features of X,' in the above example it denotes instead a nominal phrase meaning 'someone looking like X' or 'someone seeming to be X.' Thus, in this era, the suffix *-rasi-i* also expanded semantically.

Second, the suffix *-rasi-i* began to follow the past form of verbs (-*ta*). In example (47) *sikonasi-ta -rasi-i* 'very familiar' consists of the part form of the verb *sikonas-u* 'used to doing something' and the suffix *-rasi-i* (cf. Iwasaki 2013:129).

(47) *Ee **sikonasi-ta-rasi-i** nanzoi=no, iyaras-i to i-u-te tatinoki=masu to* [...]
'She felt over-friendly, so she leaves his side saying "lascivious."'
('Keisei Akatuki no Kane' *Tokugawa Bungei Ruijyu*, emphasis is mine)

Although the suffix *-rasi-i* could form a new construction in which the suffix follows the past form of verbs, its meaning is equated to that of the adjective construction that consists of a noun phrase and *-rasi-i* (i.e., look like X, seems X). Yamamoto (2010) claimed that the adjective construction with the suffix was expanded to change from a noun or nominal phrase followed by *-rasi-i* to an adnominal phrase of verbs followed by *-rasi-i*. The suffix *-rasi-i* in the construction seemed to follow the past form of verbs. Thus, they followed a finite clause. However, in the Early Middle Era, since the modern Japanese adnominal suffix *-no* had not yet been established, the past form *-ta* was used to form an adnominal phrase. Thus, the suffix *-rasi-i* did not follow the past form of a verb but instead followed an adnominal phrase, for it is reasonable for it to conform with the construction consisting of a noun phrase followed by the suffix *-rasi-i*. In the early modern era, the scope of the suffix *-rasi-i* expanded from this construction consisting of a single noun followed by the suffix to a construction that included a noun phrase followed by it. It was thus noted that the grammatical status of the suffix *-rasi-i* was in the process of change. As the process continued, the suffix *-rasi-i* came to be preceded by various types of words and phrases. Until the end of early modern era, the suffix *-rasi-i* could follow a demonstrative, as exemplified below (cf. Yamamoto 2012: 173).

(48) *Iya mou zuibun tazune=mas-u=redo=mo **sore-rasi-i** hito=ni=mo aimasen-nan=de gozari=masur-u.*
'Well, we have been looking for her, but I could not see such a woman.'
('Sanjyusannenki Tamoto no Sirasibori' *Kabuki Daityoo Syusei*, emphasis is mine)

The first appearance of the suffix *-rasi-i* had been in the Late Middle Era, and then it began to follow nominal phrases and demonstratives in the Early Modern Era. It is reasonable to argue that the adjective [X-*rasi-i*] was reanalyzed and developed into the adjective construction [[X (noun or noun phrase)]-*rasi-i*] in the Early Modern Era because a wider variety of elements could be embedded into X.

4.4.2.3. The early years of the Modern Era (1860-1945)

The evidential *-rasi-i* had rarely been used following a finite clause in the Edo Period. The construction [[finite clause]-*rasi-i*] began to be used in the early years of the Modern Era (1860-1945), its frequency increasing from around 1900 (cf. Matsumura 1977, Suzuki 1988). The evidential *-rasi-i* had already designated both the inference and hearsay parameters in the novel *Konziki-yasya* 'The Golden Demon,' which was published around 1900. In example (49a), a wife who sees her husband leaving their house all dressed up utters the sentence with suspicion. The evidential *-rasi-i* in the sentence represents the inference parameter because her suspicion is based on what she has witnessed. On the other hand, the evidential *-rasi-i* in (49b) denotes the hearsay parameter, where the owner conveys information he has heard from a couple.

(49) a. *Kesa dekake-ta=no=mo doomo ayasi-i=no,* **tasikani Hikawa=e it-tan=zya-na-i-rasi-i.** *Dakara goran=nasai. Konogoro=wa nantonaku syare-te i-mas-u=wa=ne, sousi-te kesa nanzo=wa haori kara obi made sita-te orosi zukume=de, sono kireigoto to it-ta=ra, itu=ga Hikawa=e iku=no=ni anna=ni mekasi-ta koto=wa ari=wa si=mase-n.*
'[...] There was something strange about him when he went out this morning. I don't believe he went to Hikawa. You see too how dandified he is now-a-days. This morning he had on everything new, just from the tailor, *haori*, *obi* etc. Quite a fop. He wouldn't dress himself like that to visit Hikawa. I am sure he did not go there.'
b. *Hutari=wa=no, kesa sinbun=o miru to kyuuni omoitui-te, Atami=ni dekake-ta=yo. Nandemo kinoo isya=ga* **toozi=ga ii to i-u-te sikiri-ni susume-ta-rasi-i=no=da.**
'After reading the morning paper my wife and Miya hit on the idea that they would go to Atami, and they packed and started at once; perhaps the doctor advised the hot springs for Miya.'
(Konzikiyasya 'The Golden Demon,' emphasis is mine)

The evidential *-rasi-i* in the Early Modern Era denoted both evidential parameters but was used differently from at present. First, as exemplified below, the negative form of the evidential *-rasi-i* was used to describe a woman who does not look like the kind of woman who grew up in a family that conducts a clean business. The present evidential *-rasi-i* does not have a negative form, while the suffixal usage retains a negative form (cf. Yamamoto 2012:175).

(50) '[...], *Naa Kaka,' to dooki motome-te doko=kara hippat-te ki-ta=ka* **tada=no musume=de oitat-ta-rasi-ku=wa na-ki** *kaka=ni ie=ba,* [...]
'"[...], don't you think? Wifey." said to seek for her consent to his wife, who doesn't seem to be out of character for a woman growing up in a fairly ordinary family, [...]'
('Kiku-no Hamamatu.' Rohan Zensyuu, emphasis is mine)

Second, the evidential *-rasi-i* in the Early Modern Era could modify predicates denoting that the subject has the ability to think and perceive, such as *omow-ar-er-u* (seem, appear) and *mier-u* (someone can see). These predicates are not modified by *-rasi-i*, but rather by *-yoo=ni-*, which is the adverbial form of *-yoo=da* (cf. Suzuki 1988: 49–50).

(51) a. *Sosi-te sono sugata=ga, hito=no kehai=ni odoroka-sare-te, isoi=de aga-*

roo to **suru-rasi-ku omo-ware-ta**.

'And the figure seemed to be trying to rush up, startled by the person's crawl.'

(*Seinen*, emphasis is mine)

b. *Tuini kokozo to i-u kyusyo=o **tukan-da-rasi-ku mie-ta**.*
'Finally, she seemed to find the heart of the matter.'

(*Aru Onna*, emphasis is mine)

In addition to these predicates, -*rasi-i* could also be used to modify predicates such as those shown in (52). In contemporary Japanese grammar, -*yoo=da* is used instead of -*rasi-i* to describe metaphorical meaning (e.g. *Kaze=no-yoo=ni hasir-u* vs. **Kaze-rasi-ku hasir-u* (running like a wind)), which implies that in the Early Modern Era, -*rasi-i* possibly denoted a kind of metaphorical meaning, like -*yoo=da* and -*mitai=da* do at present (cf. Yamamoto 2012: 176).

(52) *Nanananoka=ni tera=e=no husemono, boti=no tyaya=e mainiti=no tyadai, hanaryo sooziryo=nado, nanika=ni tuke-te **kane=ni=wa hane=ga hae-ta-rasi-ku tobi yuk-u**.*

'An offering to a temple for the forty-ninth day after his death, a daily tip for the teahouse, condolence gifts and dues for cleaning and so on. Money flies as if it were given wings at every moment.'

('Kyoogen Musume' *Teihon Hirotu Ryuro Sakuhinsyuu Ge*, emphasis is mine)

Finally, as stated above, the past form -*ta* had been used in the Early Modern Era to construct an adnominal phrase instead of the adnominal suffix -*no*. The adnominal makers =*no* and =*mono* then developed and took the place of the adnominal phrases formed by the past form -*ta* (cf. Yamamoto 2012: 178).

(53) *Ikuraka tame-te kaet-te kuru=kara sibaraku sinboo si-te kure to i-u-yoo=na guai=de **atti=e watat-ta=no-rasi-i**-yoosu, [...].*

'[...], probably he moved there, as if to say, please put up with this life since I earn some money there and come back here, [...].'

('Kooinga' *Rohan Zensyuu*, emphasis is mine)

Considering the emergence of the construction [[adnominal phrase] -*rasi-i*] along with the development of the adnominal marker -*no*, as was expected, it is appropriate that the example of -*rasi-i* following the past form of verbs (-*ta*) was regarded as a manifestation of the construction [[(ad)nominal phrase] -*rasi-i*]. At present, the construction that includes the adnominal marker -*no* is not used (e.g. **asita=wa atui=no-rasi-i.* vs. *asita=wa atui-rasi-i* (I heard that it would be hot tomorrow.)). However, this construction has measurable value in terms of clarifying the language change of evidential -*rasi-i*, for it could be conceived as a bridge between the suffixal construction [[X(noun)]-*rasi-i*] and the evidential usage [[finite clause]-*rasi-i*]. In short, evidential -*rasi-i* developed from the suffix -*rasi-i* that follows a noun, and then the scope of the suffix -*rasi-i* was extended from a single noun to a nominal phrase. After that, in the process of the development from the suffix -*rasi-i* to evidential -*rasi-i*, the construction [[adnominal phrase] -*rasi-i*] served as a bridge connecting them. The loss of [[adnominal phrase] -*rasi-i*] means that evidential -*rasi-i* solely followed a finite clause to form its present evidential construction [[finite clause]-*rasi-i*]. In other words, it acquired the grammatical status of an evidential marker.

The historical transition of -*rasi-i* is summarized in the following table. To put it briefly, the adjectival construction [X-*rasi-i*] was expanded into the construction [[nominal phrase] -*rasi-i*], which led to the eventual formation of the evidential construction [[finite clause]-*rasi-i*].

Table 4.8. The language change of evidential -*rasi-i*

	Late Middle (12c-16c)	Early Modern (17c-18c)	Modern (1860-)
Grammatical Category	Suffix		Evidential marker
Meaning	Typicality / Similarity		INFR / HS
Construction	[X -*rasi-i*] >	[[nominal phrase]-*rasi-i*] >	[[finite clause]-*rasi-i*]

4.5. The transition from the early years of the Modern Era to the Modern Era

Table 4.8 shows the constructional and semantic changes that accompanied the language change of evidential -*rasi-i* from the suffix -*rasi-i*. Given the paucity of previous studies that have comprehensively researching the transition of -*rasi-i* after 1900, I will investigate this topic to reveal how its evidential and suffixal usages have been utilized and to elucidate the transition they have undergone since 1900. I collected examples of the usage of -*rasi-i* whether suffixal or evidential, and compared data from two sets of novels: the first published between 1900 to 1950, and the second since 2000.

The data from novels published between 1900-1950 was extracted from the database *Aozora-Bunko Top 100*.[12] In order to focus only on Japanese expressions written by Japanese native speakers, I eliminated any data that had been translated into Japanese. To ensure that only data from the period in question was used, any data that did not have a clear year of publication was also excluded. As a result, the database contained 1084 examples that included -*rasi-i* or any of its inflected forms. The data from novels published after 2000 was collected from the category 'magazines (novels)' in the database *Balanced Corpus of Contemporary Written Japanese* (hereinafter 'BCCWJ'). To obtain an accurate picture of the contemporary usages of *-rasi-i*, I eliminated all data that had been translated into Japanese or that had been written by authors born before 1950. This left 1097 remaining in the database. In comparing the differences between the two data sets, I paid particular attention to the type of item followed by *-rasi-i* and the inflectional form taken by *-rasi-i*. First, with respect to the items followed by *-rasi-i*, I found the following variations:

(54) Items followed by *-rasi-i* in the two data sets
Formal nouns[13]
 Isi=wa   *kare=ga*   *nage-ta=**mono-rasi-i**.*
 Stone=TOP   3SG=NOM   throw-PST=FN-INFR-NPST
 'The stone seems to be thrown by him.'
Adjectives
 Yaguti=ga   *ase=reba*   *aser-u=hodo,*   *Miyabi=ni=wa*
 Yaguchi=NOM   hasty=COND   hasty-NPST=ADVP   Miyabi=DAT=TOP
 okasi-i-rasi-ku,   *warai goe=ga*   *ooki-ku*   *nar-u.*
 funny-NPST-INFR-ADV   laughter=NOM   aloud-ADV   become-NPST
 'The more Yaguchi got hasty, the more Miyabi found it to be funny and laughed aloud.'
Stems (words regarded as unanalyzable adjectives)
 Sosite omoidasi-ta-yoo=ni,   *onna=ni*   *mukat-te*   ***wazato-rasi-i***
 then   remind-PST-APP=COP.INF   woman=DAT   toward-GER   artificial-AS-NPST
 hakusyu=o   *si-ta.*
 clap=OBJ   do-PST
 'And then, as if he were reminded, he gave an artificial hand to the woman.'
Ellipsis
 '*Sore-kurai=de*   *akirameru-na=yo.*   *-**rasi-ku-nai=zo**.*'
 DIST-ADVP=COP.INF   give up-NEG=SEP   φAS-ADV-NEG=SEP
 'Do not give up with a trifling matter. That isn't like you.'
Particles
 Soo i-u   *Anzyu=wa*   *syogakkoo=kara*   *kaet-te*
 so   say-ADN   Anzyu=TOP   elementary school=ABL   back home-GER
 ki-ta=bakari-rasi-i.
 come-PST=RST-INFR-NPST
 'Anzyu said so. She seems to have just come back home.'
Pronouns
 Wakare=o   *enkyoku=ni*   *tuge-te*   *kuru=no=wa,*
 Farewell=OBJ   euphemistic=COP.INF   say-GER   come=NMLZ=TOP

  yasasii **Daiti-rasi-i**   *to=mo*   *omot-ta.*   *Doozi=ni,*
  kind   Daichi-AS-NPST QUOT=ADD think-PST. simultaneous=DAT
  sutoreeto=na   *kare-rasi-ku-na-i*   *to=mo*   *omot-ta.*
  straightforward=COP.ADN 3SG-AS-ADV-NEG-NPST QUOT=ADD think-PST
  'Although I thought it's typical of kind Daichi to say farewell to me euphemistically, I also simultaneously thought that it is not typical of straightforward Daichi to say so.'

Verbs
  Miyazaki=no *hanasi=ni* *yoru=to*   *Kido=no*   *zyugyoo=wa*
  Miyazaki=GEN story=DAT accord=COND Kido=GEN class=TOP
  Kido=ga   *tokutokuto* *hanasi-te* *ir-u*   *saityuu=wa*   *issai*
  Kido=NOM in triumph tell-GEN be-NPST middle=TOP any
  mudabanasi=wa **kinsi-s-are-te**   *ir-u-rasi-i.*
  small talk=TOP inhibit-VS-PASS-GER be-NPST-HS-NPST
  'According to Miyazaki, in the Kido's class, (the students) inhibit any babbles while he is talking in triumph.'

Negative elements
 a. *Dansi seito=no*   *aida=de=wa*   *renzoku yuukaiziken=wa*
   Men student=GEN group=COP.INF=TOP serial kidnapping=TOP
   sir-are-te   *i-na-kat-ta-rasi-i.*
   know-PASS-GER be-NEG-VBLZ-PST-HS-NPST
   'The serial kidnapping was unknown among the male students.'
 b. *Rin-san=mo* *tanin=no*   *soozyuu-sur-u* *hikooki=wa,*   *doomo*
   Ms. Rin=ADD other=GEN flying-VS-ADN airplane=TOP, seemingly
   otituka-na-i-rasi-i*=noda.*
   calm-NEG-NPST-INFR=NMLZ.COP
   'Seemingly, Ms. Rin also worried that a person who she doesn't know well handled the airplane.'

Nouns
  Koko=wa   *dooyara*   *eki=no*   **matiaisitu-rasi-i.**
  PROX=TOP apparently station=GEN waiting room-INFR-NPST
  'Here appears to be the waiting room of the station.'

Inflected forms of *-rasi-i* are shown in the following examples:

(55) Inflected forms of *-rasi-i*
End-form
 a. *Yoku* *miru=to*   *deiriguti=no* *sotogawa=de*   *Miyazaki=ga*
   closer watch=COND door=GEN externalside=LOC Miyazaki=NOM
   dada=o   ***kone-te***   ***ir-u-rasi-i.***
   tantrum=OBJ act-GER be-NPST-INFR-NPST

'Now that I look closer, Miyazaki seems to be acting like a baby outside the door.'

b. *Soto=no   kehai=ga   ugoi-te   i-ta.   Raihoosya=wa*
Outside=GEN indication=NOM change-GER be-PST visitors=TOP
hutarizure-rasi-kat-ta.
couple-INFR-VBLZ-PST

'(I) caught wind of something that changed outside. The visitors, who seemed like a couple, were approaching.'

Nominalization form

*Tuyogat-te   miser-u   **otokonoko-rasi-sa=ni**, Tatuto=wa*
brave=GER   try to be-NPST boy-AS-NMLZ=DAT Tatuto=TOP
issyun   me=o   mihat-ta.
moment   eye=OBJ   throw up-PST

'Tatuto stared in wonder at his boyish act of trying to be brave.'

Attributive form

Konoha-rasi-i   *midori iro=no   kage=ga   boyake-te   utut-te*
foliage-AS-NPST green=GEN   shadow=NOM blur-GER   reflecre-GER
ir-u.
be-NPST

'The green shadow that seems like foliage is blurry in the picture.'

Adverbial form

Oomono-rasi-ku, *tantootyokunyuu=ni   kiridasi-te   ki-ta.*
big shot-AS-ADV straightforward=DAT open her talk-GER come-PST

'Like a big-shot, she began her speech straightforwardly.'

Suspended form

*Dooyara   denwa=no   aite=wa   Masayuki=no **titioya-rasi-ku**,*
Apparently phone-GEN party=TOP Masayuki=GEN father-INFR-ADV,
kinoo=kara   kyoo=ni   kakete=no   koto=no   tenmatu=o
yesterday=ABL today=DAT span=GEN   thing=GEN   story=OBJ
kare=wa   setumeisi-te   ir-u.
3SG=TOP   explain-GER   be-NPST

'Apparently he is talking to Masayuki's father on the phone, and he is explaining the whole story from yesterday until today to his father.'

The two components are arranged in Table 4.9, which shows the data from novels published between 1900 and 1950, and Table 4.10, which is based on the data from novels that have been published since 2000. The vertical axis labels are the items followed by *-rasi-i* and the horizontal axis labels are the inflected forms of *-rasi-i*. Upon comparing the data shown in Table 4.9 and Table 4.10, it was found that the following tendencies were prevalent during the transition from the early years of the Modern Era (1900–1945) up to the Modern

CHAPTER 4 THE LANGUAGE CHANGE OF JAPANESE EVIDENTIAL -RASI-I   85

Table 4.9. The data published from 1900 till 1950

	End form	Nominalization form	Attributive form	Adverbial form	Suspended form	Total	%
Formal noun	32		1		10	43	3.97
Adjective	3			2		5	0.46
Stem	15	8	44	40	3	110	10.16
Particle	1		2		1	4	0.37
Pronoun	8		11	3	1	23	2.12
Verb	236		63	23	56	378	34.90
Negative	49		2	1	7	59	5.45
Noun	102	10	230	107	12	461	42.57
Total	446	18	353	174	92	1,083	100.00
%	41.18	1.66	32.59	16.07	8.49	100.00	

Table 4.10. The data from novels published since 2000

	End form	Nominalization form	Attributive form	Adverbial form	Suspended form	Total	%
Formal noun	40		2		1	43	3.92
Adjective	18			11		29	2.64
Stem	11		12	18	1	42	3.83
Particle	1		1		1	3	0.27
Ellipsis	2			9		11	1.00
Pronoun	9	1	14	11		35	3.19
Verb	367		40		88	495	45.12
Negative	84		4		23	111	10.12
Noun	151	4	101	41	31	328	29.90
Total	683	5	174	79	156	1,097	100.00
%	62.26	0.46	15.86	7.20	14.22	100.00	

Era (2000–).

(56) Tendencies related to the inflected forms of *-rasi-i*
    a. A decrease in the frequency of attributive forms and adverbial forms
                From 1900 till 1950   Since 2000
      Attributive forms: 32.59%   >   15.86%
      Adverbial forms: 16.07%   >   7.20%
    b. An increase in the frequency of end forms and suspended forms
                From 1900 till 1950   Since 2000

| End forms: | 41.18% | > | 62.26% |
| Suspended forms: | 8.49% | > | 14.22% |

(57) Tendencies in the items preceding -rasi-i
    a. A decrease in the frequency of nouns and an increase in that of verbs

	From 1900 till 1950		Since 2000
Nouns:	42.57 %	>	29.90%
Verbs:	34.90 %	>	45.12%

    b. A decrease in the frequency of stems (words regarded as unanalyzable adjectives)

	From 1900 till 1950		Since 2000
Stems:	10.16%	>	3.83%

    c. Ellipsis was not used in the data from 1900 till 1950, but its usage was noted in the data from after 2000.

	From 1900 till 1950		Since 2000
Ellipsis	0%	>	1.00%

Thus, the tendency (56) of decreasing frequency of attributive and adverbial forms but increasing frequency of end forms means that since 2000 the evidential usage of -rasi-i has become more frequent than the suffixal usage, because the attributive and adverbial forms were originally features of the adjective suffix -rasi-i, and the evidential -rasi-i in modern Japanese does not have such inflected forms. In other words, -rasi-i has gradually come to be used and entrenched as an evidential marker. In addition, tendency (57a) also indicates that the frequency of the evidential usage has increased because the evidential -rasi-i can follow the end form of verbs and thus have a finite clause as its scope. As regards the decreasing frequency of stems followed by -rasi-i, the adjectival construction [X(noun)-rasi-i], which had been lexicalized from the beginning, has become less frequent today. Furthermore, given the decreasing frequency of nouns followed by -rasi-i, the suffix -rasi-i could have declined in productivity in modern Japanese. Finally, ellipsis, in which the item followed by -rasi-i is omitted from the sentence, appeared in the data from novels published since 2000. The context in which the ellipsis occurs is limited to conversational sentences, however, indicating the possibility that -rasi-i is being used as a kind of discourse marker.

    As a result, evidential -rasi-i has higher productivity than its suffixal counterpart. Also, in the period of historical transition, the evidential -rasi-i that follows a finite clause had inflected forms such as attributive, adverbial and negative forms, as is the case with suffixal -rasi-i. However, those inflected forms of evidential -rasi-i have been lost. These results show that modern Japanese has been an increasingly clear distinction between the suffixal and evidential usages of -rasi-i.

4.6. The language change of the evidential -rasi-i: subjectification and de-subjectification

I have overviewed how evidential -rasi-i developed from the suffix -rasi-i. In this Section, I will describe the cognitive factors that motivated the language change of evidential -rasi-i. As reviewed in Section 2.2, Jakobson (1990) defined evidentiality through a combination of three events: speech event (E^s), narrated event (E^n), and narrated speech event (E^{ns}). Reconsidering this definition from the perspective of Cognitive grammar, the speech event in Jakobson's definition fits into the ground, and his narrated event into the process or proposition profiled in the immediate scope (IS), but the narrated speech event does not correspond to any framework in cognitive linguistic theory. I will argue that the mode of cognition proposed by Nakamura (2019) to describe a narrated speech event is a critical factor for a proper understanding of evidentiality.

4.6.1. Language change from the suffixal usage to the evidential usage

Suffixal -rasi-i [X-rasi-i] is composed of an adjective with a noun preceding it and refers to the typical feature of the referent designated by the noun. Therefore, as shown below, this construction is inflected in the same way as other adjectives in Japanese. On the other hand, evidential -rasi-i cannot be inflected, as shown in (58). It can be said that this is evidence of decategorialization because the suffix -rasi-i has lost its feature as an adjective in the transition to the evidential usage.

(58)(=3)
    a. Substantivized form -rasi-sa
       e.g.) *Kare=no   otoko-rasi-sa=ni   odoroi-ta.*
          3SG=GEN   man-AS-NMLZ=DAT   be.surprised-PST
       'I was surprised by his manhood.'
    b. Adverbial form to qualify a predicate -rasi-ku
       e.g.) *Kare=wa   otoko-rasi-ku   koodoo-si-ta.*
          3SG=TOP   man-AS-ADV   act-VS-PST
       'He acted like a man.'
    c. Negative form -rasi-ku-nai
       e.g.) *Kare=wa   hontoo=ni otoko-rasi-ku-na-i.*
          3SG=TOP   real=DAT   man-AS-ADV-NEG-NPST

'He is really not masculine.'

(59)(=19)
- a. *Dooyara,   hayame=ni syuppatu-suru   {-rasi-i   / *-rasi-sa*
    apparently   early=DAT   departure-VS   {-INFR-NPST / *-INFR-NMLZ
    / *-rasi-ku-na-i}.
    / *-INFR-ADV-NEG-NPST}
    'Apparently, they are going to leave early.'
- b. *Tanaka=ni   yoru=to,   Katoo=wa   raisyuu*
    Tanaka=DAT   accord=COND   Kato=TOP   next week
    hikkos-u   {-rasi-i   / *-rasi-sa   / *-rasi-ku-na-i}.
    move home-NPST {-HS-NPST   / *-HS-NMLZ   /*-HS-ADV-NEG-NPST}
    'According to Tanaka, Kato will move home next week.'

In addition, the adjective construction formed by the suffix *-rasi-i* can be modified by the adverbial *totemo* 'very.' In contrast, *otoko-rasi-i* in sentence (60b) with evidential *-rasi-i* cannot be modified by such an adverbial.

(60) a. *Kare=wa   totemo   [otoko-rasi-i].*
    3SG=TOP   very   [man-AS-NPST]
    'He is very manful.'
- b. *Kotira=ni   kuru=no=wa   dooyara   (*totemo)   otoko-rasi-i.*
    PROX=DAT   come=FN=TOP   apparently   (*very)   man-INFR-NPST
    'The one coming closer seems to be a man.'

The reason for this different treatment is that the two usages of *-rasi-i* have different compositions. The suffix *-rasi-i* is an adjective [X-*rasi-i*], but evidential *-rasi-i* can be decomposed into a construction 'noun plus evidential *-rasi-i*' [[X]-*rasi-i*]. This becomes clear from considering the phrase in the following sentence, where it looks like an adjective phrase. In sentence (61), in which the evidential *-rasi-i* represents the inference parameter, the phrase *kane-ni naru* 'profitable' modifies not the adjective phrase *siromono-rasi-i*, but just the noun *siromono* 'product' (cf. Yamamoto 2012: 173).

(61) *Ore=mo nandaka [[kane=ni naru siromono]-rasi-i]=kara, tyoromakasoo to omou=ga, nakanaka daizinisi-te hanasa-nee=wa.*
    'That seemed something lucrative, so I tried to sneak it. However, he wears it next his skin.'

    ('Tyuusingura Gonichi no Tatemae' *Mokuami Kyakuhonsyuu*, bracket is mine)

That is, the morpho-syntactic factor that makes the suffix *-rasi-i* change into evidential -*rasi-i* is 'rebracketing,' which is a morpho-syntactic change from a single construction [X-*rasi-i*] to a construction consisting of two sets of components [[X]-*rasi-i*]. This rebracketing is caused by a categorical judgement of an entity with which the conceptualizer has interacted. In relation to the semantic change of -*rasi-i*, the 'typical feature' meaning represented by the suffix -*rasi-i* belongs to the realm of knowledge-based information (cf. Sadanobu 2008), which can be accessed by many people. In contrast, evidential meaning, such as the inference and the hearsay parameters, is comprised of experience-based information, which can only be accessed by the people who have directly experienced a situation related to the information.

(62) *Sikitari=ni hansite=mo tadasii-koto=o ositoosu=no=ga* **wakamono-rasi-i iken** *to 'otona'=wa i-u=ni tigaina-i.*
'Adults must regard pushing own justice through against their convention as a typical youthful opinion.'

(BCCWJ, emphasis is mine)

(63) '*Syoo+Syoo omachi-kudasa-i*' *to it-te, miko=wa hasit-te ik-u. Sibara-ku-si-te* **kannusi-rasi-i** *otoko=ga de-te ki-ta.*
'"Just a moment, please." said the priestess and ran into a room. After a few moment, a man who looks like a Shinto priest came out of the room.'

(BCCWJ, emphasis is mine)

In sentence (62), which includes the suffix -*rasi-i*, *wakamono* 'young people,' the referent of the phrase *wakamono-rasi-i* refers to a prototype which can be accessed by the public who share an image of *wakamono* 'young people' in their cultural community. While on the other hand, in sentence (63) with evidential -*rasi-i*, *kannusi* 'Shinto priest,' the referent represented by the phrase *kannusi-rasi-i* is an emergent image based on the conceptualizer's interaction with an object. In fact, the conceptualizer in this situation does not have complete conviction that the object they have interacted with is a Shinto priest, but rather the conceptualizer assesses the object to be a Shinto priest based on their experience with it. In this case, the proposition 'the object is a Shinto priest' can be accessed only by the conceptualizer, because the phrase *kannusi-rasi-i* designates experience-based information. In order to reveal what cognitive factors drove the language change, it is necessary to describe the semantic and conceptual difference between suffixal and evidential -*rasi-i*. Langacker's subjectification framework (cf. Figure 3.2(c)), however, is inadequate to explain these differences, since what is required is a configuration that reflects the assessment of speakers based on their experience of and interaction with the objects in question and the environment around them.

In this respect, I argue that the formulation of evidentiality requires 'the narrated speech event' propounded by Jakobson (1990). This can be understood from the fact that the tense marker is marked twice in a sentence with Japanese evidentials, as shown in (64). In the sentence *eito torakku-ga donnamono-ka-mo sira-nai-rasika-tta*, the evidential *-rasi-i* is marked with the past tense marker *-ta*, but the sentence followed by *-rasi-i* is marked as present tense. The sentence has the structure [[*eito torakku-ga donnnamono-ka-mo siranai*]-*rasi-kat-ta*].

(64) '*Boku=ga unten=o hazime-ta koro=wa eito torakku dat-ta.*' *to Iehuku=wa it-ta. Misaki=wa nanimo iwanakat-ta=ga, dooyara hyoozyoo=kara-sur-u=to eito torakku=ga donna mono=ka=mo siranai-rasi-kat-ta.*
'"Eight-track tape was used to listen to music in a car when I had begun to drive." said Iehuku. Misaki did not say anything. Judging from her expression, she did not know what the eight-track is like.'

(Onna no Inai Otokotati, emphasis is mine)

The evidential *-rasi-i* here is marked as past tense because it describes a narrated speech event, where the speaker can obtain the information from the source to be able to infer that the narrated event 'She doesn't know an 8-track tape' was an event prior to the speech event. However, considering the timeline of the story, the narrated event is marked with present tense to represent that it occurs concurrently with the narrated speech event, though not at the same time as the speech event. In other words, this demonstrates that in addition to a speech event and a narrated event, a narrated speech event is also necessary in order to formulate evidentiality.

Below I will summarize the constructional and semantic features of suffix and evidential *-rasi-i*. The phrase with the suffixal usage of *-rasi-i* is used as an adjective construction as a whole and sketched in Figure 4.2. It is the same configuration as in Figure 3.2(a) used by Langacker (1990) for describing lexical items, where G is not included in the MS, meaning that the G is not in the scope of awareness and thus less conscious in the conceptualization.

(a) (b)

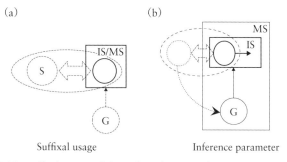

Suffixal usage   Inference parameter

Figure 4.2. The suffixal usage and the evidential usage (inference parameter) of -rasi-i

More importantly, I added the interaction between conceptualizer and referent as an object of conception, illustrating it by an ellipse and a double-headed arrow with a broken line to indicate that the I-mode cognition is functioning behind Langacker's viewing arrangement when we conceptualize something. The typical feature of X represented by *X-rasi-i* has been abstracted from the interaction with X in the physical, social and cultural environment, called 'simulation' (cf. Barsalou 1983). Therefore, the interaction unconsciously functions behind a referent coded by language when we conceptualize something. The inference parameter represents that an unknown referent A invokes the conceptualizer as a reminder of a conception X with which we are already familiar, based on the cognitive image emergent in their interaction with referent A. As sketched in Figure 4.2, in this case the ellipse drawn with a broken line represents the narrated speech event, in which the conceptualizer interacts with an entity in the environment, and G is in the MS since their assessment based on their experience is coded. The configuration is broadly the same as in the figure showing deictic elements and grounding elements given by Langacker (1990) (cf. Figure 3.2(b)). To indicate that the assessment is based on their experiential interaction, I have included the I-mode cognition in Langacker's figure.

Although the process from suffixal *-rasi-i* to evidential *-rasi-i* designating the inference parameter does not fit into any of the instances of subjectification proposed by Langacker, it is reasonable to say that the process fits into the framework of subjectification in the sense that the subject of conception comes into the MS in the transition and functions as the reference point for their judgement of the event's reality. In other words, the sentence with evidential *-rasi-i* is included in their assessment. In addition, it is noteworthy that the subjectification is driven by the conceptualizer's interaction with the entity and its environment. That is to say, the de-subjectification proposed by Nakamura drives the subjectification in relation to the language change of evidential *-rasi-i*.

4.6.2. The emergence of the hearsay parameter from the inference parameter

My research has revealed that hearsay cannot be marked with the past tense. Considering that the suffixal usage and the evidential usage denoting the inference parameter can also be marked with the past, it can be said that the hearsay parameter is more grammaticalized than the inference parameter owing to loss of its lexical features. As pointed out earlier, the evidential *-rasi-i* that denotes the hearsay parameter has the following differences from the evidential *-rasi-i* that denotes the inference parameter. First, if the evidential *-rasi-i* is placed after a conditional clause in a sentence, it cannot be interpreted as 'inference,' but can rather only be naturally understood to be 'hearsay,' as shown in (65) and (66). Second, propositions based on inference cannot be canceled by speakers themselves, while those based on hearsay can be, as exemplified by (67).

(65)(=6)
Mosi asita   ame=ga   hut-ta=ra,
if   tomorrow rain=NOM   fall-PST=COND
undookai=wa   tyuusi=ni   naru-rasi-i.   [*Inference/Hearsay]
sports day=TOP suspension=DAT   be-HS-NPST
'If it rains tomorrow, the sports day will be called off.'

(66)(=7)
Taro=no   hanasi=de=wa,   [Mosi asita   ame=ga
Taro=GEN   story=COP.INF=TOP   [If   tomorrow   rain=NOM
hut-ta-ra,   undookai=wa tyuusi=ni   naru]-rasi-i.   [Hearsay]
fall-PST-COND sports day=TOP suspension=DAT be]-HS-NPST
'Taro told me, "If it rains tomorrow, the sports day will be called off."'

(67)(=8)
  a. *??Asioto=ga   sur-u.   Dareka=ga   heya=ni   hait-te*
     Footstep=NOM do-NPST someone-NOM   room=DAT enter-GER
     ki-ta-rasi-i=ga,   watasi=wa soo omowa-na-i.   [Inference]
     come-PST-INFR-NPST=ADVRS   1SG=TOP   so   think-NEG-NPST
     'I hear footsteps approaching. Someone may come into the room, but I don't think so'
  b. *Sensei=no   hanasi=de=wa,   taro=wa   kaze=de*
     Teacher=GEN   story=COP.INF=TOP   Taro=TOP   cold=CSL
     kesseki-rasi-i=ga,   watasi=wa soo omowa-na-i.   [Hearsay]
     absence-HS-NPST=ADVRS   1SG=TOP   so   think-NEG-NPST

'Our teacher said that Taro was absent because he got a cold, but I don't think so.'

These differences can be explained in terms of the difference in layering structure between the inference parameter and hearsay parameter. Taking (66) as an example, the sentence with evidential -*rasi-i* denoting the hearsay parameter exhibits a multiple-layered construction similar to that of a complex sentence (e.g. [*Taro-ga* [*mosi asita ame-ga hut-ta-ra undookai-wa tyuusi-ni nar-u*] *to hanasi-ta*] ([Taro told me that [the sports day would be called off if it rained the next day]])). The construction with the hearsay parameter denoted by -*rasi-i* differs from the construction of a complex sentence in the sense that the subject of conception is not encoded as the subject of the main clause. Although the subject is unspecified, the hearsay parameter implicates that the part followed by -*rasi-i* represents not the speaker's assessment but information that someone conveyed to the speaker. In other words, it is the speaker that assesses the finite clause that is followed by the evidential -*rasi-i* designating the inference parameter, but the part followed by the evidential -*rasi-i* denoting the hearsay parameter is information the speaker conceives of as being originally thought or assessed by someone else. Therefore, the main factor driving the semantic change of evidential -*rasi-i* is an increase in the number of conceptualizers, as shown in Figure 4.3.

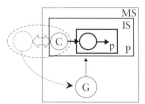

Figure 4.3. Hearsay parameter

This figure indicates that the speaker (G) conceptualizes the proposition (P) in which someone else (C) conceptualizes the process (p). Both the inference parameter and the hearsay parameter represent the indirect access to the event that the finite clause followed by -*rasi-i* designates. However, the conceptualizer in the sentence with the inference parameter corresponds to the speaker because it is based on interaction with an entity and its environment. On the other hand, the sentence with the hearsay marker has two conceptualizers, the speaker and the narrator who told the information to the speaker, having the structure [the speaker assesses [that someone else assesses [the event]].

As to the factors giving rise to the layering construction, I assume that 'intersubjectivity,'[14] meaning our ability to read each other's minds, functions as part of our general cognitive ability. The most important factor is the hearer's role in understanding the uttered expression, as represented by the hearsay parameter. To understand the uttered expression and apply the hearsay parameter, the hearer must deduce from the speaker's utterance the existence of a conceptualizer who does not correspond to the speaker. The hearer needs to read the speaker's mind, which facilitates the formation of a conceptual layering construction [the speaker construes [the other construed [proposition]]]. In sum, though I have stated that the factor driving the semantic change from evidential *-rasi-i* to the hearsay parameter is an increase in the number of conceptualizers, this increase is inevitably motivated by the conceptual layering construction based on intersubjectivity.

Notes

1. This suffixal usage includes unanalyzable adjectives like '*ahorasi-i* (nonsense)' and '*nikutarasi-i* (hateful)'.
2. The evidential *-rasi-i* has an adverbial form *-rasi-ku*. However, it is not used to modify a predicate but only as suspended form (e.g. *Dooyara han'nin-wa zyoosyuuhann-rasi-ku, syouko tonar-u mono-wa nokosi-te ina-kat-ta*. 'The perpetrator seemed to be a habitual criminal because he had left without any telltale marks.').
3. Regarding 'empirically based assessment,' Miyake (2006) stated that it is not inference but rather recognition of evidence that some entity exists. However, he did not discuss the definition, and the difference between them remains unclear. For the reasons, I saw no problem in regarding 'empirically based assessment' as belong to the same category of Aikhenvald's (2004) inference parameter.
4. The term scope is 'the general term that we shall use to describe the semantic "influence" which such words have on neighboring parts of a sentence.' (Quirk et al. 1985: 85)
5. Koyanagi (2013a, 2013b) divided the process of language change into 'the production of function words' and 'the systemization of grammar.' Table 4.2 shows the producing functional words.
6. In Old Japanese, the ending form and attributive form of predicates had been distinguished morphologically. However, the morphological distinction was lost around the Late Middle Era.
7. The evidential *-soo=da* in modern Japanese was originally pronounced *-sau=na* in the Late Middle Japanese.
8. While Senba (1972) stated that the evidential *-gena* following a finite clause had arisen in the Muromachi period (16th century), Aoki (2007) claimed that it had arisen in Kamakura period (14th century).
9. *-gena* as evidential usage can also be used as a collocation [*-ta-gena* (want + EV)] (e.g. *Kare=wa Nanika ii-ta-gena yoosu=de watasi=o mi-ta*. 'He looked at me as if he seemed to be tell me something.')
10. Senba (1972) presented that there are examples of the evidential *-soo=da* denoting the inference parameter in *Ukigumo* written by Futabatei Shimei in the Meiji period, which means that the evidential *-soo=da* denoting the inference parameter still existed into the Meiji

period.
11 Some scholars have pointed out that the evidential *-rasi-i* is derived from the evidential marker *-rashi* designating the inference parameter in Old Japanese. However, their claims are doubtful for the following two reasons: i) the evidential marker *-rasi-i* in Old Japanese fell into disuse in the Late Middle Era, ii) the evidential *-rasi-i* in modern Japanese arose only after the suffixal usage had arisen (cf. Asakawa and Takebe 2014: Ch 23). Considering these two facts, the evidential *-rasi-i* in Modern Japanese does not have a direct connection to the earlier form. Even supposing the two forms to be related, it is appropriate to predict more likely that the evidential *-rasi-i* in modern Japanese developed from the evidential *-rasi-i* of Old Japanese via the suffixal usage. Therefore, it is reasonable to examine the grammaticalization path from the suffixal usage to the evidential usage of *-rasi-i* in Modern Japanese.
12 'Aozora-Bunko Top 100' is a database collected from well-trafficked novels ranked in the top 100 of all 'Aozora-Bunko' titles.
13 The data included '*-tumori* (e.g. 1900–1950: 7 / 2000–: 14)', '*-koto* (e.g. 1900–1950: 1 / 2000–: 12)', '*-mono* (e.g. 1900–1950: 32 / 2000–: 11)', '*-ki* (e.g. 2000–: 3)', '*-sei* (e.g. 2000–: 1)', '*-tokoro* (e.g. 1900–1950: 2 / 2000–: 1)', and '*-no*(e.g. 1900–1950: 1)'.
14 The term 'intersubjectivity' is defined as follows: the term 'intersubjectivity' denotes our presumption that the other exists in the world as a subject of conception in the same manner as ourselves, and the other conceives the existence of the same world as we ordinary conceive it. (cf. Takeda 2005: 132).

CHAPTER 5

How evidentiality is expressed in novels

5.1. Introduction

In Section 2.5, I overviewed the argument about the relationship between evidentiality and epistemic modality and concluded that they are not the same categories at all. Instead, the two categories play complementary roles, which are performed when humans make judgements about the reality of a situation described by a speaker. In this chapter, I argue that it is the relative predominance of one of these categories over the other that gives rise to a difference of 'fashion of construal' between Japanese and English. It is worth noting that there is a tendency to use words related to evidentiality in novels provided in Japanese and English, as exemplified by (1) and (2). Both of the sentences in (1) contain an expression related to evidentiality. The evidential marker *-rasi-i* indicates that the inference parameter is used in the Japanese sentence, while the adverb *perhaps* is used to denote the inference parameter in the English.[1] However, even though the evidential *-rasi-i* denotes the inference parameter in the Japanese sentence, no evidential meaning is marked at all in the English one (2).

(1) *Langudon=wa heddosetto=o kansatusi-ta. Sore=wa yuubina kyokusen=o egak-u kinzoku=no bando=de, ryoohasi=ni tiisana paddo=ga tui-te ir-u=-dake=da.* **Komat-ta kao=ni kizui-ta-rasi-ku**, *uketukegakari=ga tetudai=ni ki-ta.*
'Langdon eyed the headset, which was nothing but a sleek loop of metal with tiny pads at each end. **Perhaps seeing his puzzled look**, the young woman came around to help him.'

(*Origin*, emphasis is mine)

(2) *Baatendaa=wa gurasu=o mitasi=nagara, kagami=de yoosu=o mitei-ta. Syookoo=ga gamen=ni ni, sando hure-te=kara keitaidenwa=o mimi=ni ater-u.* **Aite to tunagat-ta-rasi-ku**, *hayakuti=no supeingo=de it-ta.*

'As the barmaid refilled the thugs' glasses, she watched in the mirror as the officer touched a few keys on his phone and then held it to his ear. **The call went through,** and he spoke in rapid Spanish.'

(*Origin*, emphasis is mine)

From the perspective of CG, both sentences in (1) designate an event regarded as irreal by a conceptualizer by marking the expression as belonging to the inference parameter of evidentiality. This shows that each conceptualizer in both languages references the event in a manner that denotes uncertainty about its occurrence. In contrast, the English sentence in (2) is not marked by any items that denote the event as irreal, though the Japanese one is marked by *-rasi-i*, which designates the inference parameter. Hence, Japanese and English speech differ in terms of their construal of the reality of an event, even when describing the same situation.

I will examine why this difference arises by incorporating the 'narratology' framework into cognitive linguistic theory. In novels, the characters experience various events in the story, but the way the story is told depends on the speaker who tells the story. The distinction between character and narrator could be a crucial factor in explaining the differences related to the use of evidentiality. From the perspective of the CG theory, the different tendencies in the marking of evidential meaning in novels between Japanese and English can be analyzed in terms of the different fashions of construal that are typical of the two language. In other words, Japanese evidential *-rasi-i* can be used in a situation narrated through subjective construal. It therefore describes the scene experientially. In contrast, English has a more limited capacity to express a situation experientially, so speakers feel less need to employ elements designating evidential meaning.

5.2. Cognitive linguistics and narratology

As explained in Chapter 3, cognitive linguistics, especially Langacker's theory, analyzes language based on a conceptual substrate where the subject of conception construes the object of conception. While the object of conception is profiled in the on-stage region and encoded in linguistic expression, the subject of conception and its construal are implicit off-stage and ground the expression as a reference point.

CHAPTER 5   HOW EVIDENTIALITY IS EXPRESSED IN NOVELS   99

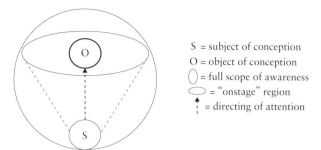

S = subject of conception
O = object of conception
◯ = full scope of awareness
⌒ = "onstage" region
↑ = directing of attention

(Langacker 2008: 260)

Figure 5.1. Conceptual substrate (= Fig.3.1)

In ordinary language use, the speaker becomes the subject of conception, but when we analyze language expressions in novels, we have to consider that the subject of conception can be either a character who experiences several events in the story, on the one hand, or a narrator who relates these events to the reader, on the other.

5.2.1. The narrator and focalizer in the framework of narratology

Genette (1972) pointed out a confusion in the traditional narratological approach toward the framework of viewpoint between 'who sees?' and 'who tells,' distinguishing between the former as related to 'focalization' and the latter as related to 'narration.' He defined three categories based on the relationship between character and narrator.

Table 5.1. Genette (1972)'s three types of focalization

zero focalization	narrator > character	The narrator knows more than the characters or, more exactly, says more than any of the characters knows.
internal focalization	narrator = character	The narrator says only what a given character knows.
external focalization	narrator < character	The narrator says less than the character knows.

The three categories are based on the regulation of information, which arises from the choice of a restrictive vantage point. With 'zero focalization' the narrator knows more than the character, being regarded as omniscient. 'Internal focalization restricts the narrator to say what a given character in the narrative world knows and is used in situations where the narrator states their own internal feelings or talks about an event that the character perceives in the narrative world. 'External focalization' constrains the narrator to say less than the character knows. As a result, the reader of the narration can visualize a situation that is similar to that of the character without ever knowing the character's thoughts or feelings. No singular focalization is consistently adopted, but rather different focalizations are adapted depending on the scene in question.

According to Genette's theory, describing an event perceived from the vantage point of a character in the narrative world falls under the category of internal focalization. However, the situation can also be analyzed through external focalization of the event by the character. Therefore, his theory could have difficulty in determining which type of focalization is most applicable to an expression. Bal (1985: 105) added the differentiation between subject and object of focalization to Genette's framework, calling the subject of focalization the 'focalizer' and the object the 'focalized.' The subject and object of focalization are exemplified as follows (cf. Hashimoto 2014):

(3) *Chieko to Shin'ichi=wa kisi=o megut-te, kogurai konositamiti=ni hait-ta. Wakaba=no nioi to, simet-ta tuti=no nioi=ga si-ta. Sono hosoi konositamiti=wa mizikakat-ta. Mae=no ike=yori=mo hiroi ike=no niwa=ga, akaruku hirake-ta. Kisibe=no benisidare=no sakura=no hana=ga, mizu=ni=mo utut-te me=o akaruku-suru. Gaizin=no kankookyaku-tati=mo, sakura=o syasin=ni tot-te i-ta.*
'Walking around the bank, Chieko and Shin'ichi entered a small path in the shadow of some trees. It smelled of young leaves and damp earth. The narrow, shaded path was short; where it ended, a bright garden opened up beside a pond that was larger than the previous one. The flowers of the red weeping cherry trees were reflected in the water and flashed in the eyes of the visitors. Some foreign tourists were photographing the blossoms.'

(*The Old Capital*)

In the first sentence *Walking around the bank, Chieko and Shin'ichi entered a small path in the shadow of some trees*, the characters *Chieko* and *Shin'ichi* are referred to in the third person. The actions of the characters (the focalized) are told from the perspective of the narrator (the focalizer). The second sentence *It smelled of young leaves and damp earth*, on the other hand, is described from the perspective of the characters. In this case, the characters are the focalizers who perceive the event (*It smelled of young leaves and damp earth*) and convey it through their vantage point.

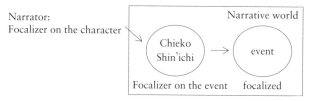

(Hashimoto 2014: 195)
Figure 5.2. The relationship between focalizer and focalized

In other words, the first sentence represents the configuration of external focalization, in which a narrator outside the narrative world perceives the characters' actions in the narrative world. In the second sentence narrated with internal focalization, on the other hand, the event experienced by the characters is described from the viewpoint of the characters in the narrative world.

5.2.2. Fashion of construal: the two types of construal

The Sapir-Whorf hypothesis claimed that each language has its own 'fashion of speaking.' Consequently, even if describing the same situation, speakers of different languages can adopt different language expressions (cf. Whorf 1956). According to cognitive linguistic theory, a language reflects how its speakers conceptualize the world. Cognitive linguistics argues that if language expressions can differ across languages despite representing the same situation, and if these language expressions reflect different conceptualizations of the world, 'fashion of speaking' is equal to 'fashion of conceptualizing the world.' Ikegami (2006, 2013) coined the term 'fashion of construal' to refer to a way of conceptualizing the world and, claiming that there are both universal and particular, language-specific aspects to fashion of construal (Ikegami 2013: 626).

(4) **The universal aspect in languages**
Every language speaker has the ability to construe events in different ways and encode a given event using different expressions.
The relative aspect between languages
Speakers of different languages can have different preferences in the construals they adopt, even though representing the same event.

In the case where the event being spoken of is the existence of windows in a room, the fashion of speaking can be different in Japanese and English. In Japanese, it is natural to refer to the event using *ar-u* 'be,' as shown in (5a). In contrast, it is more natural in English to use *have*, as shown in (5b). The two languages also each have another choice to describe this situation: Japanese verb *motu* 'have' and English the construction *there is/are* (e.g. *There are two windows in the room.*). Therefore, it is reasonable to suppose that the difference is caused by the speakers' preferences in the construals they adopt.

(5) [Talking about the windows in a room]
    a. *Kono*   *heya=ni=wa*   *mado=ga*   *hutatu*   *ar-u*.
        PROX   room=DAT=TOP   window=NOM   two   be-NPST
    b. *This room has two windows.*

(Ikegami 2006: 161)

Based on the 'fashion of construal' assumption, Ikegami (2011) and Hamada (2014) pointed out that there is a difference in construal between Japanese and English.

(6) **Subjective construal vs. objective construal**
Subjective construal: The speaker is located within the very same situation she is to construe and construes it as it is perceivable to her. Even if she is not located within the situation she is to construe, she may mentally displace herself into the situation she is to construe and construes it as it would be perceivable to her. The speaker, who construes the situation, is embedded in the very same situation she is to construe and her stance here is characterizable as "subject-object merger."
Objective construal: the speaker is located outside the situation she is to construe and construes it as it is perceivable to her. Even if she is embedded in the very same situation she is to construe, she may mentally displace herself outside the situation she is to construe, leaving, however, her counterpart behind - in other words, the speaker undergoes a self-split here, herself stepping out of the situation but at the same time, leaving her counterpart behind in the situation. The speaker, who construes the situation, is detached from the situation she is to construe and her stance here is characterizable as "subject-object contrast."

(Ikegami 2016: 304)

(7) Conceptualizer's vantage points and conceptualization of events
    (A) Japanese and Korean speakers have a strong tendency of construing an event through their conventionalized view which results from the vantage point within the setting in which the event unfolds and describe it by activating their reference point ability.
    (B) English speakers have a strong tendency of construing an event outside the setting objectively and describe it according to the figure / ground organization.

(Hamada 2014: 12)

In sum, Japanese speakers prefer 'subjective construal,' which means that they experience and express an event as they feel it in the situation. On the other hand, English speakers prefer 'objective construal.' Thus, they view an event with a bird's-eye view and express it as outside observers. For example, in the opening scene of the novel *Yukiguni* 'The Snow Country,' the scene where the character is on a train is described as follows.

(8) *Kokkyoo=no   naga-i   tonneru=o   nuker-u=to*
    border=NOM   long-NPST   tunnel=OBJ   come out of-NPST=COND
    yukiguni=de   a-tta.
    snow country=LOC   be-PST
    'The train came out of the long tunnel into the snow country.' [(translated by) E. Seidensticker]   (Ikegami 2006: 195)

In the English sentence, *the train* is overtly described. This means that the narrator is relating the scene as perceived from outside of the train. In the Japanese sentence, in contrast, the train is not overtly described, which means that the narrator is relating the scene as perceived from inside of the train.

If we accept the idea that the different languages have different fashions of speaking, it is not difficult to assume that examples of such differences can be found in the parallel translation of novels. That is, speakers of Japanese are preferential to 'subjective construal,' which tends to utilize internal focalization to express what the character experiences in the narrative world. On the other hand, since speakers of English prefer 'objective construal,' external focalization by the narrator is more likely to be used to describe an event from outside of the narrative world.

5.3. Comparing evidential *-rasi-i* in Japanese with its counterparts in English

In this section, I will first present the data to be examined in my study. Following that, I will focus on examples in which there are differences between Japanese and English in the coding of evidential meaning, and then present my explanations for why these differences arise. The data was collected from six novels written in both English and Japanese. Novels I, II and III were originally written in English and novels IV, V and VI were in Japanese. All of the novels were translated by a different translator. To collect the data, I first collected expressions with the Japanese evidential *-rasi-i* from the Japanese edition of the four novels, and then collected their counterparts from the English versions. Table 5.2 shows the results of the survey, and the instances of each category are aggregated in Table 5.3.

(9) The list of novels from which the data was collected

	Author	Title	Translator
I.	Brown, Dan.	*Origin.*	Echizen, Toshiya
II.	Ishiguro, Kazuo.	*The Buried Giant.*	Tuchiya, Masao.
III.	Kirn, Walter.	*Up in the Air.*	Eguchi, Taiko
IV.	Minato, Kanae.	*Kokuhaku.*	Snyder, Stephen
V.	Nakamura, Fuminori	*Suri.*	Izumo, Satoko and Coates, Stephen
VI.	Murakami, Haruki	*Hitsuji-o Meguru Booken.*	Birnbaum, Alfred

Table 5.2. English expressions corresponding to the evidential -*rasi-i* in Japanese

Category	Example	I	II	III	IV	V	VI	Total
Subjunctive mood	as though, as if		1		1		1	3
like	like, look like, sound like	3		4	2	7	1	17
Verb	seem, feel	2	1	2			2	7
Verb + infinitive	appear to-, seem to-	9	1		1		2	13
Verb + that S V	appear that-, think that-, seem that-, read that-, told me that-, sense that-, claim that-, convince that-, see that-, say that-, suppose that-, occur that-, mean that-, hear that-	9	6	23	8	3	1	50
adverbials	perhaps, clearly apparently, supposedly according to, probably	24	1	7	2	2	7	43
unmarked	∅	7	9	13	3	6	7	45
non-evidential modification	(Adjective)	3	2	1				6
Relatives	(received) word that -, rumor that -	1			1			2
Modality	must	1		1			1	3

Table 5.3. Classification of the evidential -*rasi-i* and its correspondents in English

Subjunctive mood	There was a furtive mood among them, as if they were keen their words were not overheard even by those in their own ranks, and Axel could see hostile glances exchanged.	*Onmitu muudo=ga sihaiteki=de, nani=o hanas-u toki=mo kogoe=da. Sorezore=ni zibun=no kotoba=ga syuui=ni morekikoe-nai=yoo ki=o tuka-te ir-u-rasi-kat-ta.*
like	'Looks like you're quite a hero.' The man tugged on one of Ávila's most prized emblems.	'*Nakanaka=no eiyuu-rasi-i=zya-na-i=ka.*' *Toku=ni kityoona kisyo=o hippar-u.*
Verb of perception	Tonight, however, Ambra's indiscretions seemed all but forgotten. The	*Sikasi kon'ya, Ambra=no muhunbetu=wa sukkari wasure sara-re-te simat-ta-rasi-i.*

+ infinitive	tidal wave of media activity generated by the events in Bilbao had swelled to an unprecedented magnitude.	Birubao=de=no zitai=de syozi-ta hoodoo gassen=no oonami=wa kuuzen=no kibo=ni hukure agat-ta.
+ infinitive	As he padded farther down the passage, Langdon finally saw the end - a black curtain barrier where guests were being greeted by doctors who handed each of them **what appeared to be a thick beach towel** before ushering them through the curtain.	Tuuro=o sara=ni susumu=to, yooyaku tukiatari=ga mie-ta - Anmaku=no kakat-ta iriguti=de gaido=ga kyakutati=o mukae, **atude=no biiti taoru-rasi-ki mono**=o tewatasi-te=kara, anmaku=no mukoo=e annaisi-te ir-u.
+ that S V	'I see. Recently, **I read that for the first time in Harvard's history, the incoming student body consists of more atheists and agnostics than those who identify as followers of any religion.**	'Naruhodo. Saikin nanika=de yonda=no=da=ga, **haavaado=no rekisi=de hazime-te, zibun=ga kirisutokyoto=da=to kangaeru nyugakusei=yori=mo, musinronzya ya hukatironzya=no nyugakusei=no hoo=ga ooku=nat-ta-rasi-i.'**
adverbials	**Apparently this afternoon's match had gone the way of Ireland's visiting team.**	Dooyara, gogo=no siai=de Airurando=kara ki-ta tiimu=ga zyoo+zyoo=no kekka=o dasi-ta-rasi-i.
Unmarked	As the barmaid refilled the thug's glasses, she watched in the mirror as the officer touched a few keys on his phone and then held it to his ear. **The call went through**, and he spoke in rapid Spanish.	Baatendaa=wa gurasu=o mitasi=nagara, kagami=de yoosu=o mi-te i-ta. Syooko=ga gamen=ni ni, sando hure-te=kara keitaidenwa=o mimi=ni ater-u. **Aite to tunagat-ta-rasi-ku**, hayakuti=no supeingo=de it-ta.
Non-evidential modification	As Köves moved through the wide portico of this once grand city residence, he passed through a doorway inscribed with **an encoded message:**	Kebessyu=wa katute doodootaru tosizyutaku=dat-ta tatemono=no hiroi yanetuki genkan=ni hairi, toguti=o nuke-ta. **Doa=ni angoo-rasi-ki mono**=ga sirus-are-te ir-u.
Relatives	He had just received **word that Uber was experiencing difficulties tracking the shooter's getaway car.**	Sakki=no denwa=ni yoru=to, **sogekihan=no toosoosyaryoo=no tuiseki=ni uubaa=wa tekozu-tte ir-u-rasi-i.**
Modality	This is your self-portrait? Langdon glanced again at the collection of uneven squiggles. **You must be a very strange-looking computer.**	Kore=ga zigazoo=dat-te? Langdon=wa hukinkoo=de zonzaina e=ni mooitido me=o yatta. **Kimi=wa zuibun hentekona sugata=no konpyuutaa-rasi-i=na.**

The results reveal that the most frequent English counterparts to the Japanese evidential *-rasi-i* were verbs and adverbials indicating evidential meaning. In contrast, the modal auxiliary was rarely used only three times. It should be noted that instances of the evidential being unmarked in English were observed in all six novels. The results show that differences in the encoding of evidential meanings between Japanese and English can be analyzed in terms of the two languages' different fashions of speaking, rather than merely reflecting the preferences of the translators themselves.

5.4. The difference in the encoding of evidential meanings between Japanese and English

As we have noted, the encoding of evidential meanings can differ between Japanese and English. In particular, I have focused on the fact that an expression encoding evidential meaning with evidential *-rasi-i* in Japanese can be translated into an expression that has no evidential markers in English. The examples are divided into two types of situations in the data I collected. The first type is a situation where the character perceives an event. This falls under the inference parameter, based on what the character has perceived. As shown in (10), the barmaid saw the officer making a call using a phone and speaking in Spanish. She inferred from the officer's action that the call had gone through. In example (11), the character in the gallery heard footsteps approaching him and inferred from the sound that someone had entered the gallery.

- Type 1: A situation where the character perceives an event
(10) (=(2))
> *Baatendaa=wa gurasu=o mitasi=nagara, kagami=de yoosu=o mi-te i-ta. Syookoo=ga gamen=ni ni, sando hure-te=kara keitaidenwa=o mimi=ni ater-u.* **Aite to tunagat-ta-rasi-ku**, *hayakuti=no supeingo=de it-ta.*
> 'As the barmaid refilled the thug's glasses, she watched in the mirror as the officer touched a few keys on his phone and then held it to his ear. <u>The call went through</u>, and he spoke in rapid Spanish.'
> <div align="right">(<i>Origin</i>, emphasis is mine)</div>

(11) *Sotogawa=no dokoka=de doa=no ak-u oto=ga si-te, kibi+kibi-si-ta asi-oto=ga takai kabegosi=ni hibi-ta. Sakki, tikaku=ni mie-ta doa=kara,* **dareka=ga tenzisitu=ni hait-te ki-ta-rasi-i.**
'A door clicked somewhere outside, and brisk footsteps echoed beyond the high walls. <u>Someone had entered the gallery</u>, coming through the nearby door that Langdon had seen.'
(Origin, emphasis is mine)

The configuration of type 1 is illustrated below. The character in the narrative world is described in the third person, and the same character also perceived the event. Therefore, we need to describe the situation in terms of a dual structure. The first structure is a configuration where the narrator (focalizer 1) is external to the narrative world and focalizes on the character (focalized 1). The second one is a configuration where the character (focalizer 2) in the narrative world focalizes on the event (focalized 2).

CHAPTER 5 HOW EVIDENTIALITY IS EXPRESSED IN NOVELS 107

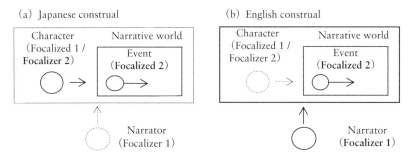

Figure 5.3. The Japanese and English construal in type 1

In this type, the difference between Japanese and English depends on the type of 'focalization' that was adopted. In the Japanese expression, the character in the narrative world inferred the event from what they could perceive (e.g. the officer's action and the sound of footsteps), because the character's experience is inevitably needed to encode the inference parameter. Therefore, it can be said that the narrator said only what the characters know, which means that the situation was narrated using internal focalization. In this way, what the character can know is limited to the information they can perceive in the narrative world. When they describe an event they cannot access directly, one requiring information that transcends their perception or knowledge, some marked expression such as a marking modal or adverbial is needed to describe the situation as an irreal event. Nonetheless, the English expressions in (10) and (11) were expressed without any markers representing the inference meaning. This shows that the narrator knows more than the characters and presents the information as real. Thus, the expression was described using zero focalization from the perspective of the narrator external to the narrative event.

The second type of case in which Japanese evidential -*rasi-i* is left untranslated in English is a situation where a character tells another character in the narrative world information that was conveyed to them by others. In this case, the hearsay parameter of evidential -*rasi-i* is used in the Japanese expression. For example, as shown in (12), when the character is asked about the incident by the police officer, he conveys information that he heard from the automated docent. In (13), an old woman tells her husband about the information she received from a strange woman. Both Japanese sentences are marked with evidential -*rasi-i*, while the English equivalents are expressed without any evidential items.

- Type 2: A situation where a character conveys information received from others
(12) '*Dare=ni keikoku-sare-ta?*' *Yozire-te katamui-ta heddosetto=ga hoho=ni atat-te ir-u.* '*Kono heddosetto=ga Edomondo Kaasyu=no konpyuutaa=ga keikokusi-te ki-ta=n=da, syootaikyaku risuto=ni husinna zinbutu=ga not-te ir-u to.* **Taieki-si-ta supein=no syookoo-rasi-i.**
'"Warned by whom?!" Langdon could feel his transducer headset twisted and askew on his cheek. "The headset on my face . . . It's an automated docent. Edmond Kirsch's computer warned me. It found an anomaly on the guest list - <u>**a retired admiral from the Spanish navy**</u>."'

(*Origin*, emphasis is mine)

(13) '*Kitto omae=no sinsetu=ni kansya-si-te ir-u-daroo=yo, ohimesama. Zuibun nagaku hanase-ta=no=kai*' '*Ee.* **Mukoo=mo hanasu koto=ga takusan at-ta-rasi-ku-te.**' '*Kokoro=o midasu-yoo=na koto=o iw-are-ta-mitai=da=-na, ohimesama. Mura=no onnatati=ga i-u=toori, tikazukanai hoo=ga ii onna=dat-ta=no-kamo-sire-na-i.*'
'"She would have been grateful for your kindness, princess. Did you speak long with her?" "<u>**I did and she had a deal to say**</u>." "I can see she said something to trouble you, princess. Perhaps those women were right and she was one best avoided."'

(*The Buried Giant*, emphasis is mine)

The configuration of type 2 is basically equivalent to that of type 1, but it contains more complex layered structures embedding the meta-narrative world[2] in the narrative world since the character is conveying their narrative story to others. Therefore, the character acting as focalizer 1 in the narrative world narrates an event in the meta-narrative world where the character who is focalizer 2 obtained the information of the proposition (focalized 2) by interacting with yet another, who was the source of information. The relationship between the character in the narrative world and the one in the meta-narrative world in the type 2 configuration parallels the relationship between the narrator and the character in the type 1 configuration.

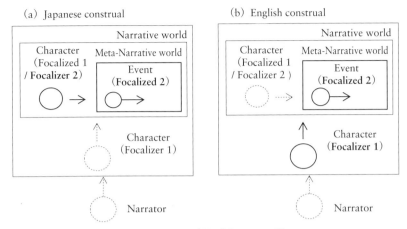

Figure 5.4. Japanese and English construal in type 2

Japanese and English also differ in the focalizations that are utilized in the two languages. In the meta-narrative world, the character as focalizer 2 (e.g. Langdon in (12), and the old wife in (13)) obtains the information (e.g. a retired admiral from the Spanish navy in (12), and she had a deal to say in (13)) by interacting with another (e.g. an automated docent in (12), a strange woman in (13)), who is the source of the information. Consequently, the character in the meta-narrative world cannot directly access the reality of the information owned by the other. Accordingly, when information that the character cannot access directly is described, the expression is marked to represent the event as irreal for the character. In fact, evidential *-rasi-i* was used in the Japanese expressions, which means that the character in the meta-narrative world was playing the role of focalizer 2. In the Japanese case, the narrated information is based on what the character in the meta-narrative world obtained. Thus, the character in the narrative world said only what the character in the meta-narrative world knows, for the situation was narrated using internal focalization. On the other hand, as is the case with type 1, the English sentence is expressed without any markers that make up evidential meaning. A possible reason for this is that, since the meta-narrative world is not the focus of the interaction with the other, the information obtained there takes on the quality of a real entity that the character in the narrative world has come to know. The character in the narrative world conveys it as real, so the character in the meta-narrative world cannot access it directly, which means that the character in the narrative world says more than the character in the meta-narrative world knows. Hence the situation was narrated using zero focalization.

5.5. The cognitive factor reflected in the different markedness of evidentiality

As was shown in Table 5.2, the result of the survey shows that the modal auxiliaries in English are seldom used as the translation of Japanese evidential *-rasi-i*. This indicates the possibility that the inference parameter of evidentiality does not belong to the category of epistemic modality. In addition, as I discussed in Section 5.3, regarding the factors behind the difference in the markedness of the items representing evidential meaning, I showed that the expressions in Japanese are expressed by using internal focalization, while the ones in English are expressed by using zero focalization. My contention parallels the conclusions of Ikegami (2006, 2016) and Hamada (2016), both of whom indicate that Japanese speakers are more likely to construe an event from within the very same situation they are construing, while English speakers prefer to construe an event outside the situation. In sum, Japanese speakers need to mark evidential meaning when they describe information they cannot access directly, because they have a penchant for construing an event from the vantage point of the character in the narrative world (or meta-narrative world). In contrast, the English speakers do not feel the need to use any markers of evidential meaning, because of their tendency to construe an event from the perspective of narrator outside the narrative world (or meta-narrative world). As Ikegami (2014) pointed out, the difference is a matter of fashion of speaking, for both languages have other ways to describe the event.

In the relation to fashion of construal, Honda (2005), through comparative studies of direct and indirect quotes and of mental predicates such as those referring to feeling and thinking, concluded that Japanese speakers tend to use 'empathetic constructions,' while English prefers 'transparent constructions.' In sum, the other's feeling can be seen directly by the speaker in English, but in Japanese it is treated as obscured from the speaker (Honda 2005: 168). Japanese mental predicates are limited to a first-person subject, while English has no such restriction and can also choose a third person subject, as shown in (14). In (15), the verb *want*, which represents the subject's intention, is used as the main predicate in the English sentence, but the direct quote marker *-tte* is used in the Japanese translation.

(14) a. I am sad.
    b. *Watasi=wa kanasi-i.*
    c. He is sad.
    d. **Kare=wa kanasi-i.*

(Honda 2005: 168)

(15) Tom=ga   anta=to   hanasi-tait-te.
    Tom=NOM   2SG=COMIT   talk-DES-DQ
    'Tom wants to talk to you.'

(Honda 2005: 166)

According to Honda (2005), a direct quotation is a kind of expression that shows a reconstruction of another's speech based on the speaker's assumptions. To reconstruct the other's speech, we need to read the other's intention empathetically, which means that the speaker must construct expressions as if they were the one who made the original statement. Besides, a sentence with the verb *want* in English describes a situation as if the speaker were construing the event as an omniscient being.

Previous studies related to fashion of construal have explored the differences that can be found across various languages at both the grammatical and expressional levels. The difference shown by Honda (2005) is related to grammatical differences, such as person restrictions in mental predicates and the direct quotative, in which the relationship between the speaker and the grammatical subject is examined. Thus, if the subject is in the third person, their feelings and thoughts are obscured from the speaker. I have showed that the fashion of construal at the level of grammar and expression is parallel to the use of evidentiality in narratives. The focus is on the relationship between the narrator outside the narrative (or meta-narrative) world and the character in the narrative (or meta-narrative) world. The Japanese narrator and the speaker in the narrative world empathetically construe an event from the perspective of the character in the narrative (or meta-narrative) world. Hence, when the event cannot be accessed directly by the character in the narrative (or meta-narrative) world, marking by evidential *-rasi-i* is needed to represent the inference based on the source of information that the character perceived or obtained. On the other hand, the English narrator and speaker in the narrative world construe an event outside the narrative (or meta-narrative) world transparently. Therefore, a situation expressed with evidential *-rasi-i* in Japanese is described without any markers of evidential meaning in English. In this way, by introducing frameworks from narratology, it becomes evident that examples of evidential meaning being encoded in Japanese but not in English can be explained by differences in fashion of construal at the narratological level. This study has thus concluded that when the narrator or the speaker in the narrative world narrates a situation which was construed empathetically (i.e. with internal focalization) by a character in their narrative world, the Japanese evidential *-rasi-i* is marked in the description, but no marker of evidential meaning is used in the English translation of these sentences. This indicates that the Japanese evidential *-rasi-i* is colored by an interpretation of subjective construal, whereas English is less affected by the subjective construal reflected in evidential meaning.

Notes
1 The English adverb *perhaps* and verbs *seem* and *appear* represents the inclination phase (cf. Langacker 2009: Chapter 9–10).
2 A meta-narrative world is a world told by a character in the narrative world (cf. Genette 1972, Hashimoto 2014). The narrated world is different from the narrating one. Therefore the narrated world precedes or follows the narrating world. In the case of a sentence with the evidential *-rasi-i*, the meta-narrative world told by the character in a narrative world is based on the character's experience, so it is understood that the meta-narrative world must precede the narrative world.

CHAPTER 6
The extension of meaning into mirativity in the Japanese evidential marker *-rasi-i*

6.1. Introduction

Evidentiality is a linguistic category that refers to the source of information (Aikhenvald 2004). Although a combination of evidentiality and a first-person pronoun is seldom seen, non-firsthand evidentiality such as the inference parameter and the hearsay parameter typically acquire mirative meanings, especially in combination with first-person terms, a phenomenon called 'the first-person effect' (Aikhenvald 2012). In this chapter, I claim that the combination of Japanese evidential *-rasi-i* and the first-person pronoun can be regarded as a mirative strategy since this combination represents finding oneself as one's new self.

Japanese evidential marker *-rasi-i* has been investigated from the aspect of its semantic features and its difference from other evidential markers in Japanese. However, no studies have focused on the extension to mirative meaning. I will incorporate the framework of cognitive linguistics, especially the conception of reality and the self to describe how evidential *-rasi-i* acquires mirative meaning in combination with first-person pronouns. In the following sections, I overview the relationship between evidentiality and person, and then introduce a model based on the mode of cognition proposed by Nakamura (2016) and on Honda's (2013) affordance theory. Such a new model is needed because Langacker's well-known reality model, which attempts to describe the conception of reality, is insufficient to describe the appearance of mirative meaning through the combination of evidential *-rasi-i* and first-person pronouns. In Section 6.4, I show data collected from expressions containing evidential *-rasi-i* along with a first-person pronoun and divide the cases into the two categories of ecological self and interpersonal self taken from affordance theory. Both represent finding oneself as one's new self through experience against the speaker's expectation. Therefore, it can be said that evidential *-rasi-i* in combination with a first-person pronoun acquires a mirative meaning in the sense that the two categories based on affordance theory designate information new to the speaker and counter expectation. As the conclusion of this study, this fact that evidential *-rasi-i* in combination with a first-person pronoun acquires a mirative meaning indicates that evidential *-rasi-i* reflects a process of conceptual formation based on interaction with an entity in the environment, namely I-mode cognition, and that even the conception of the self is formed through this process. Assuming that the cycle of awakening is reflected in evidential *rasi-i*, the mirative extension is reasonably explained by adding the difference of profiling. Thus, a conceptualizer which interacts with an object is profiled to express mirative meaning while an object with which a conceptualizer interacts is profiled to express evidential meaning.

6.2. Evidentiality from the perspective of the theory of territory

Evidentiality is closely related to person. As exemplified below, the subject of the mental predicates that represent the subject's feeling and mental state is restricted to the first-person, for it is unnatural when the subject is referred to using second or third person pronouns. According to Ikegami (2004), the English sentences corresponding to Japanese sentences with mental predicates below sound perfectly natural.

(1) a. *(Watasi=wa)*   *samu-i / atu-i.*
           1SG=TOP   cold-NPST / hot-NPST
     b. ?? *Anata=wa*   *samu-i / atu-i.*
           2SG=TOP   cold-NPST / hot-NPST
     c. ?? *Kare / Kanozyo=wa*   *samu-i / atu-i.*
           3SG=TOP   cold-NPST / hot-NPST

(Ikegami 2004: 1)

(2) a. *(Watasi=wa)*   *uresi-i / kanasi-i.*
           (1SG=TOP)   glad-NPST / sad-NPST
     b. ?? *Anata=wa*   *uresi-i / kanasi-i.*
           2SG=TOP   glad-NPST / sad-NPST
     c. ?? *Kare / Kanozyo=wa*   *uresi-i / kanasi-i.*
           3SG=TOP   glad-NPST / sad-NPST

(Ikegami 2004: 2)

This indicates that in Japanese, the speaker can refer to their own private aspects such as their senses, feelings or emotions, but cannot designate another's private aspects without foundation.

Kamio (1991) referred to the relationship between person and evidentiality as an instantiation of his theory of territory. In his theory, Japanese predicates are divided into two forms: the direct form and the indirect form. The direct form is defined as the end-form of the main predicate with an added honorific. In contrast, the indirect form is defined as the main predicate in addition to items denoting inference, hearsay, and the speaker's subjective judgement (cf. Kamio 1991: 16), as shown below.

(3) Direct form:
    a. *Kyoo=wa   yoi   tenki=des-u.*
       Today=TOP nice weather=COP.HON-NPST
       'The weather is nice today.'
    b. *Kinoo=wa   11 kiro=mo aruki-masi-ta.*
       Yesterday=Top 11km=ADD walk-POL-PST
       '(I) walked 11km yesterday.'
    c. *Yosida-kun=ga   yuube   ie=ni   yat-te   ki-masi-ta.*
       Mr. Yoshida=NOM last night house=DAT visit-GER come-POL-PST
       'Mr. Yoshida came to my house last night.'
    d. *Wa=ga   gun=wa   dankotosi-te   kussi-na-i.*
       1SG=GEN team=TOP determinedly-GER give ground-NEG-NPST
       'Our team never give ground.'

                                                        (Kamio 1991: 16)

(4) Indirect form:
    a. *Ano   hito,   dokoka   waru-i-mitai.*
       DIST man,   something wrong-NPST-INFR
       'That man looks something wrong.'
    b. *Kanozyo=wa   tabun   kur-u-daroo.*
       3SG=TOP   probably come-NPST-INFR
       'She will probably come.'
    c. *Asita-wa   harerun-zyanai=no.*
       tomorrow-TOP clear up-EPI=SEP
       'It will clear up, won't it?'
    d. *Zousyoo=no   zinin=wa   zikan=no mondai to*
       finance minister-GEN resign-TOP time-GEN matter QUOT
       omow-are-mas-u.
       think-PASS-POL-NPST
       'I think that the resignation of the finance minister is a matter of time.'

                                                        (Kamio 1991: 16)

The two forms are divided based on whether the information belongs to the speaker's territory or the hearer's territory. The direct form in (5a) indicates that the information is in the speaker's territory, while the indirect form in (5b) designates that the information is external to the speaker's territory.

(5) a. *Sensei=wa   sangatu=de   yamer-u=yo.*
       teacher=TOP   March=LOC   resign-NPST=SEP
       'The teacher is going to resign next March.'
    b. *Sensei=wa   sangatu=de   yamer-u-rasi-i=yo.*
       teacher=TOP   march=LOC   resign-NPST-HS-NPST-SEP
       'I heard that the teacher was going to resign next March.'

(Kamio 1991: 17)

The two forms are used differently on the principle of his theory of not saying anything 'against the appropriate relationship of their territory' (Kamio 1991: 219). Thus, evidential *-rasi-i* was categorized as an indirect form which refers to information external to the speaker's territory. Hence, it must not be used to represent information in the speaker's territory.

In his theory, information about a speaker, such as their birthday, is considered to belong to the speaker's territory because it is information extremely familiar to them. If this is so, then information about the speaker should be expressed by using the direct form, not the indirect form. However, it can sometimes be appropriate to designate information about the speaker by using the indirect from. In the following examples, evidential *-rasi-i* is used even though the information is about the speakers themselves. The bold sentence in (6) is uttered by a woman who finds herself feeling love toward a man she had seen like a phantom after her corneal transplant operation. The bold sentence in (7) is uttered by an old woman who has just been informed that she has a grandchild by her son who had not seen her for a long time.

(6) (Chiaki arrives at her home.)
    Chiaki's father: *Chiaki, doosi-ta=n=da?*
                    'Chiaki!? What's wrong?'
    Chiaki: *... Otosan...Atasi...moodame=yo...*
                    'Dad... I can't take it anymore...'
    Chiaki's father: *Nani=ga dame=nan=da=ne?*
                    'Can't take what?'
    Chiaki: **Atasi ano hito=ga suki=ni nat-te simat-ta-rasi-i=no.**
                    'I think I've fallen in love with him.'
    Chiaki's father: *Ano hitot-te dare=da?*
                    'Who's "Him"?'

Chiaki: *Atasi=no me=ni utur-u ano maborosi=no hito=yo.*
'The phantom I keep seeing.'

(*Black Jack*, emphasis is mine)

(7) '*Soso. Iki-te ir-u zinan.*' *Roozyo=ga ago=o hik-u.* '*Dene, tui konoaida, denwa=ga at-ta=no.*' '*Onsinhutuu=de=wa-na-kat-ta wake=ka.*' '*Honno issyuukan mae. Nizyuunen buri=ka=na, kyuuni denwa=ga at-te, sore=de=ne,* **watasi=ni=wa mago=ga ir-u-rasi-i=no***.*'
'"Exactly. My second boy who is still alive." The old lady nodded. "And there was a phone call for me from him just recently." "You are out of contact with him, aren't you?" "Only a week ago. He called me out of the blue for the first time in twenty years and **he said I have a grandson**."'

(*Sinigami no Seido*, emphasis is mine)

Kamio (1991) did not discuss these examples which present information about the speakers themselves by using the indirect form. In this chapter, I propose that these examples arise from the development of mirative meaning of evidential -*rasi-i* in combination with a first-person pronoun.

6.3. Mirativity as a general cognitive phenomenon

As seen in our overview of previous studies in Section 2.6, there are various ways to represent mirative meaning in different languages. From the perspective of cognitive linguistics, according to which meaning resides in conceptualization, mirative meaning can also be considered as a general cognitive phenomenon. The point crucial to the argument in this chapter is the nature of the cognitive phenomenon reflected in mirative meaning. In this chapter, I introduce several frameworks of cognitive linguistics. First are two frameworks to describe our conception of reality: the reality model proposed by Langacker (2009) and the construing of reality based on Nakmaura's (2016) cognitive mode. The other framework is that of two types of self: one the self as conception, and the other as directly perceived self. Finally, I relate the cycle of awakening proposed in Section 3.5 to these frameworks.

6.3.1. The conception of reality

In the conception of reality proposed by Langacker (2009), as shown in Figure 3.6, the assessment of the reality of an event is described differently depending on whether the process (p) is included in the conceptualizer's reality (D) or not. The presence of a modal is illustrated as an inclination phase, where C inclines toward accepting p as part of C's reality. Its absence is illustrated as a result phase, where the p is already established in C's dominion. The traditional terms of possibility and necessity are depicted as part of a different description and the length of the arrow represents C's commitment to the proposition (cf. Langacker 2009: Ch 5).

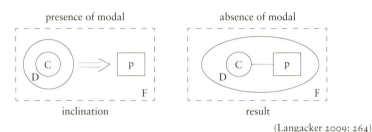

(Langacker 2009: 264)

Figure 6.1. Reality model (= Fig. 3.6)

This reality model indicates that our conception of reality is a conceptual structure into which we incorporate a proposition. Therefore, it does not describe a cycle that includes the collapse and reconstruction of reality. In addition, the conceptualizer in this model functions as the center of structuring the conception of reality, because the 'new self' is difficult to describe in this model. Considering these points, it is difficult to explain the mirative extension of evidential *-rasi-i* in combination with a first-person pronoun by using the reality model proposed by Langacker.

As another approach to the conception of reality, Nakamura (2016) defined a conception of reality by incorporating his mode of cognition:

(8) If we regard a situation as a cognitive image constructed through the I-mode cognition, we treat the situation as irreal, on the other hand, if we perceive a situation without a process of constructing a cognitive image through the I-mode cognition (i.e. the situation just perceived in D-mode cognition, we treat the situation as real.

(Nakamura 2016: 35)

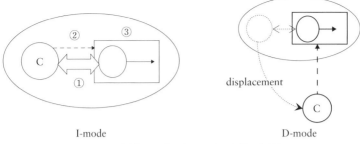

I-mode   D-mode
Figure 6.2. The mode of cognition (=Fig. 3.10)

In sum, the conception in which the I-mode cognition remains behind is regarded as irreal. On the other hand, the conception without I-mode cognition is conceived as real. Taking 'the sun rises' as an example, it was a moral certainty for medieval people who believed that the sun revolved around the earth. When the Copernican theory defied their common wisdom, however, they then realized it to have been merely an illusion that they had taken to be real. Although the Copernican revolution changed their belief from real to irreal, they needed the D-mode cognition where they employed analytic and scientific thinking to accept the new fact that the event 'the sun rises' merely appeared to be real to them. Thus, Figure 6.3 shows an intermediate phase between I-mode cognition and D-mode cognition. If a given situation that we conceptualize takes place against the background of I-mode cognition where we construct our own cognitive image, the situation is regarded as irreal, while the situation is treated as real if it is conceptualized using a scientific view without the process of I-mode cognition.

6.3.2. The two kinds of conception of the 'self'

The conceptual substrate called 'viewing arrangement,' where the subject of conception (S) chooses and focuses on its object of conception (O), lies at the foundation of CG theory (cf. Figure 3.1). The relationship between the subject and object of conceptualization is characterized in an asymmetrical fashion. When the speaker conceptualizes themselves, we assume that the configuration includes two types of self: the conceptualizer and conceptualized. The speaker as conceptualizer construes a conceptualized version of himself, though both are the same person. In relation to the configuration, Langacker (1985) incorporated the following examples of the 'split self' in his viewing arrangement.

(9) a. Don't lie to me!
    b. Don't lie to your mother!

(10) a. That's me in the middle of the top row.
   b. In my next movie I play a double-agent. Both the CIA and the KGB are trying to kill me.

(Langacker 1985: 127)

The vantage point of the conceptualizer is not always an actual one. We can assume a virtual vantage point to describe ourselves. The referents designated by *me* and *your mother* are the same person in (9). Utterance (9b) is used by a mother to caution her son not to lie from the viewpoint of the son. The viewpoint of the son is distinct from an actual one, for it is an assumed vantage point that is used by her to describe herself. In contrast, the self as an object of conception can be assumed as a virtual entity. The expressions in (10) refer to imaginary selves whom they point at in a picture or talk about as a role played in a movie, marking both with the first-person pronoun. Thus, the subject of conception can conceptualize a virtual self as the object of conception and separate it from the actual vantage point when we express ourselves with a first-person pronoun. In whichever case, the use of a first-person pronoun implies a configuration where a conceptualizing self as the subject of conception construes a conceptualized self as the object of conception.

As with Langacker (1985), Honda (2005) stated that the first-person pronoun is an expression representing the objectified speaker, who has split away from the actual speaker as a referent included in the conceptualizer's field of awareness. Meanwhile, he also proposed another conception of self, the 'directly perceived self,' thereby incorporating affordance theory. The 'directly perceived self' was divided into two types: 'ecological self' and 'interpersonal self.' They differ from the self that is represented by the first-person pronoun.

(11) **The self in affordance theory**
   a. Ecological self: the self that is perceived through interaction with entities in an environment.
   b. Interpersonal self: the self that is perceived in relation to others in an environment.

Both are perceived in a binary relation (e.g. self - thing or self - person) in developmental psychology (cf. Tomasello 1999). Linguistically, they are not marked with any items overtly. Examples are provided below (Honda 2013: 201).

(12) **Ecological self**
   When we are riding on a train toward Tokyo and perceive that the city is approaching, then we perceive our self as moving toward Tokyo.

(13) **Interpersonal self**
   If we smile at someone and they return a smile, we recognize that they regard our existence as meaningful.

When moving toward Tokyo by train, Japanese speakers sometimes state that Tokyo is approaching. However, Tokyo itself never moves. The expression can be understood since it looks like Tokyo is approaching when we perceive ourselves, the directly perceived self, moving toward Tokyo. In relation to others, we can directly perceive ourselves when others respond to our actions. The directly perceived selves proposed by Honda (2005, 2013) are not encoded. Therefore, it is reasonable to consider that they are not the self who is conceptualized in Langacker's viewing arrangement, but the self who interacts with an environment in Nakamura's I-mode cognition.

6.3.3. The relationship between the cycle of awakening and mirativity

As seen in our review of previous studies in Section 2.6, mirative is a linguistic category which represents counter- or un-expected information. In this chapter, I reveal how evidential *-rasi-i* takes on mirative meaning. First, it is noteworthy that the mirative meaning in this case arises in a particular situation where the speaker herself related her own information by using indirect evidential *-rasi-i*. Thus, evidential *-rasi-i* itself represents inference or hearsay categorized in indirect evidentiality, but the construction comprised of evidential *-rasi-i* with a first-person pronoun describes mirative meaning parasitically in the context where the speaker presents her own information obtained from the outer world. More importantly, I am approaching the question of how mirative meaning arises from the perspective of cognitive Linguistics. The fundamental principle of cognitive Linguistics is that meaning resides in conceptualization. Therefore, my goal in investigating mirative meaning is to reveal the cognitive phenomenon reflected in the mirative meaning residing in the construction parasitically.

Considering the mode of cognition proposed by Nakamura (2016), as introduced in Chapter 3, I claim that it is appropriate to employ the 'cycle of awakening' framework to describe the mirative extension of evidential *-rasi-i*. The cycle begins with the phase shown in the following Figure 6.3(a), where we treat daily cognitive experiences unconsciously and automatically. For example, we never mind which foot we should lift first when walking. Since we are not conscious of the division between the subject and object of conception when we treat experience unconsciously and automatically, we cannot decide whether an event is real or irreal in this phase. However, we sometimes experience a collapse of unconscious cognition when we sense something wrong with our habitual activities. This phase is illustrated in Fig 6.3 (b), in which our habitual cognition coexists with an analytic perspective on everyday things that we had until then taken for granted. Thus, it reflects the existence of unstable multiple perspectives when the assumptions we had taken for granted are defied. The unstable multiple perspectives, as sketched in Figure 6.3 (c), are reversed by sharing the situation with others and are thereby entrenched in our knowledge as a new perspective regarding the world.

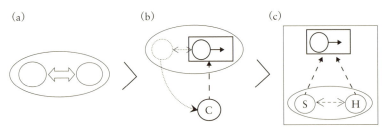

Figure 6.3. The cycle of awakening (=Fig. 3.12)

According to the usage-based model of cognitive linguistics, a novel expression and the construal reflected in it are entrenched as our conception through the actual usage events (Langacker 1999a). The conception of reality is also regarded as a set of propositions that the conceptualizer has accepted as real (Langacker 2009). In addition to the process of acquiring conceptions, the cycle that I demonstrated includes the process of the collapse and reconstruction of our conceptual reality in the usage-based model.

6.4. The extension to mirative meaning as the first-person effect of Japanese evidential -*rasi-i*

I collected data from *The Balanced Corpus of Contemporary Written Japanese* (BCCWJ). I chose expressions with evidential -*rasi-i* at random from the data from amongst literature that has been published since 2000. Of the resulting 2044 examples in the database, the examples in combination with a first-person subject are shown below.

Table 6.1. Examples of evidential -*rasi-i* in combination with a first-person pronoun

Maximum examples: 2044		
First-person subject	Overt	23
	Covert	13
Total		36

There are 23 examples of -*rasi-i* in combination with an overtly marked first-person subject. In 13 additional examples, the subject was determined to be a first-person pronoun based on the context. Considering the ratio, the use of evidential -*rasi-i* in combination with a first-person pronoun is less common. Examining the data, the examples of evidential -*rasi-i* in combination with a first-person pronoun can be categorized into two types based on the 'directly perceived self' proposed by Honda (2005).

- **The type based on Ecological self**
(14) *Koko=wa ittai doko=nan=da... Huan=ga tukiage-te kur-u. ... Sonna-hazu=wa na-i... Otituk-e! Otituku=n=da! Issyun, osorosii zyookyo=ga atama=ni ukabi awate-te hurihara-u. Hurueru yubisaki=de atari=no yoosu=o kakuninsi-te mir-u. Watasi=o torimai-te ir-u kabe=ga ki=de deki-te ir-u-rasi-i koto=ga wakat-ta.* **Dooyara, watasi=wa ki=de deki-ta hako=no naka=ni ir-u-rasi-i.**
'Where am I?... my anxiety is rising more and more. ... That can't be true... Relax! Get grip of myself! In that moment, a frightening situation comes up to mind, but I shake the feeling in haste. I touch my surroundings with my unsteady fingertips. I've found the wall surrounding myself made of wood to the touch. **Apparently, I am in a box made of wood.**'

(BCCWJ, emphasis is mine)

- **The type based on Interpersonal self**
(15) *Pati+Pati to danro=no honoo=ga hazer-u oto. Hukasigina zikan=dake=ga byookizami=de keika-si-te ik-u. '...Ano' Taekirezu=ni ore=ga kutibi=o kir-u to, Imada=wa hui to sisen=o soras-u. 'Danro=no tikaku=wa kiken=nan=de, amari tikayora-na-i=de kudasa-i=yo' 'Ah, aa'* **Ore=wa kono otoko=ni yoppodo kiraware=te ir-u-rasi-i.** *Sooto=sika kangae-rare-na-i.*
'I hear the sound of fire in a fireplace. An enigmatic time has passed by the second. "... you know." I break the ice impatiently. Imada reuses eye contact with me abruptly. "It can be dangerous around the fireplace, so keep away from it, please." "Oh, I see." **Obviously, he hates me so much.** No other idea.'

(BCCWJ, emphasis is mine)

The type based on the ecological self represents a self who is recognized through their interaction with an environment. As exemplified by (14), the character in the narrative world understood that he was in a wooden box after he had interacted with his environment by touching the wall around him. On the other hand, the type based on the interpersonal self designates a self who achieves recognition through interaction with the others.[1] For example, in the sentence in bold in example (15), the character understood how the others perceive him through communication with them. The commonality between both the ecological and the interpersonal self is that they seek to discover a new version of themselves through interaction with their environment or with others. Therefore, the mirative meaning extended from evidential *-rasi-i* in combination with a first-person pronoun can be illustrated similarly to the process from Figure 6.3 (a) to Figure 6.3 (b) in the cycle of awakening.

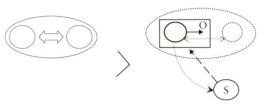

Figure 6.4. The emergence of mirative meaning

The ellipse in Figure 6.4 shows the field in which the interaction with an environment or others takes place. We interact with an environment around ourselves unconsciously: when we start to walk and open a door, we are not particular aware of a physical movement. Likewise when we are walking down a street, we do not concern ourselves with what others around us thinking. When we feel something different in our reality in daily life, we focus on that one thing. The feeling of strangeness gives rise to the unexpectedness and counter-expectation expressed by mirativity. Through the interaction depicted as a double-headed broken arrow, the subject of conception (S) recognizes the new self (O), as illustrated using a bold box. Compared with the configuration of the inference parameter of evidential *-rasi-i* in Figure 4.2 in Chapter 4, the mirative meaning shown in Figure 6.4 differs in which entity in the dotted ellipse is profiled. The profiling describes the conceptualizer's finding of a new aspect of herself through interaction with her environment or with others. In other words, an object with which a conceptualizer interacts is profiled to express evidential meaning, whereas a conceptualizer which interacts with an object is profiled to express mirative meaning.

In this chapter, I claimed that the Japanese evidential *-rasi-i* in combination with a first-person pronoun acquires a mirative meaning as an instantiation of mirative strategy (Aikhenvald 2004, 2012) because the expression represents the finding of a new self through interaction with the environment or with others. As I stated in my discussion of the relationship between epistemic modality and evidentiality, I agreed with the position that they should be distinguished (cf. Akihenvald 2004, DeHaan 1999). From the perspective of cognitive linguistics, if epistemic modality and evidentiality can be distinguished both semantically and functionally, the construal reflected in these two categories should be different as well. The reality model proposed by Langacker is appropriate for analyzing the epistemic modal by positing a proposition from within or from outside the conception of reality. In Section 3.5, I showed the cycle of awakening as another aspect of the reality model. With the assumption that the cycle is reflected in Japanese evidentiality, it can be reasonably explained that the evidential -*rasi-i* in combination with a first-person pronoun acquires a mirative meaning. That is to say, the evidential and its mirative extension reflect the cognitive process of collapsing and reconstructing our conception of reality through our experiential interaction with the environment or with others.

Notes

1 The collected data included 15 examples based on the ecological self and 21 examples based on the interpersonal self.

CHAPTER 7

Conclusion

By analyzing the behavior and historical development of Japanese evidential *rasi-i*, this book has presented an argument that a proper understanding of evidentiality can be achieved through an application of the perspective of cognitive linguistics, but only with modifications and additions to existing frameworks. After introducing the three key issues in question in Chapters 1 and 2, I went on to discuss these in depth in Chapter 3. I showed how frameworks of cognitive linguistics have been applied to explain evidentiality, and where necessary proposed modifications to these to create my own frameworks to better explain the behavior of evidentials. In Chapter 4, I discussed how evidential *-rasi-i* developed from its suffixal usage. As first noted in Section 2.4, there are two types of grammaticalization of evidentiality worldwide: development from a lexical item to a grammatical evidential, and development from evidentiality strategies. The Japanese evidential *-rasi-i* is a special case, however, being unlike either of these. I concluded that in order to explain how Japanese evidential *-rasi-i* developed from its suffixal usage, we need to incorporate not only the subjectification proposed by Langacker (1990) but also the 'de-subjectification' proposed by Nakamura (2016), since a proper understanding of its language change depends on the concept of the collapsing and reconstructing of our conceptions, a concept that the traditional configuration of subject-object contrast has difficulty in describing.

A second issue I addressed was the relationship between evidentiality and epistemic modality. In Section 2.5, I provided an overview of the different stances toward this relationship, which can be divided loosely into three positions, namely that they are to be viewed as i) the same category, ii) partially overlapping categories, or iii) completely different categories. I concluded that the cognitive functions of evidentiality and epistemic modality complement each other to arrive at judgements about the reality of the situation described. As an example to demonstrate this fact, in Chapter 5 I investigated how words related to evidentiality are used in novels in Japanese and English. As a result, I claimed that the two categories (i.e, indirect evidentiality vs. epistemic modality) represented different aspects of our conception of reality. Concretely speaking, the subjective construal advocated by Ikegami (2016) and Hamada (2014) was reflected in evidentiality because the conceptualizer assessed the reality of the perceived event within the very situation they were to construe. Considering that the evidential meaning was not expressed in English, the construal did not necessarily need to be encoded in English.

As the third issue, I examined why mirative meaning arises when evidential -*rasi-i* is combined with a first-person pronoun. As noted in Section 2.6, Aikhenvald (2004) pointed out that the expression can represent additional meaning when indirect evidential markers are expressed in combination with first-person pronouns. I especially focused on why mirative meaning arises in combination with the first-person pronoun. In Chapter 6, based on the reason that evidential -*rasi-i* in combination with a first-person pronoun describes finding a new self, I chose the case of the evidential -*rasi-i* as an example and examined the reason why mirative meaning arises from evidential -*rasi-i* from the perspective of CG. To explain why mirative meaning arises, the 'directly perceived self' must interact with an environment. Mirative meaning results from the cognitive process of the speaker finding a new aspect of themselves as the directly perceived self and then reconstructing their conception of self. The concept of the cycle of awakening introduced in Section 3.5 enables us to give a satisfactory explanation of why evidential -*rasi-i* in combination with the first-person expresses a mirative meaning. In other words, the mirative meaning of evidential -*rasi-i* in combination with first-person pronouns is supportive evidence that the cycle of awakening is exactly reflected in evidential -*rasi-i*.

The mental universe represented by language expressions is not unaltering but rather a repetitive cycle of collapsing and reconstructing. In this book I argued that such a dynamic cycle is salient in evidentiality, especially in the Japanese evidential -*rasi-i*. The study presented here has the potential to contribute to two areas of research, namely cognitive linguistics and linguistic typology. The frameworks of cognitive linguistics have constructed on the basis of phenomena in English. Though these frameworks have proven applicable to various language phenomena in English, when we try to apply them to phenomena in other languages, it is only natural that they may require refinement or modification. I investigated evidentiality, which is lacking from the grammatical system of English, by applying existing cognitive linguistic frameworks with minor modifications. In that sense, my study broadened the range of application of CG theory and showed its efficacy with regard to evidentiality. As for the contribution to linguistic typology, evidentiality was examined from the following three perspectives:

(1) i.   What kind of evidentiality exists in the world?
    ii. How are evidential meanings encoded morpho-syntactically?
    iii. Where did evidentiality come from?

Although I investigated the development of evidential *-rasi-i* in Chapter 4, I can confidently state that this book is a clear departure from previous studies of evidentiality because it considered a cognitive motivation related to the use of evidential *-rasi-i*, its language change and its extension to mirative meaning from the perspective of cognitive linguistics.

Through this book, I consistently claimed that our mental universe as presented by language expressions is a cycle of collapsing and reconstructing based on our embodied interactions with an environment, and that this cycle is reflected in the Japanese evidential *-rasi-i*. Evidentiality is defined as the source of information for utterances. On closer examination of evidential *-rasi-i* in its various aspects, we find that this definition as source of information is closely bound up with cognitive ability to conjure up a representation based on our interactions with the environment. Finally, although this book focused on the evidential *-rasi-i* in particular, Japanese has other and newer evidential markers even today. Additionally, many other languages in the world possess evidential markers. I am conscious that further studies are needed to reveal whether the cognitive ability I showed in this book can be observed in other evidential markers in Japanese and other languages. I would like to consider this question in the future.

References

Aikhenvald, Alexandra. Y. (2004). *Evidentiality*. Oxford: Oxford University Press.

Aikhenvald, Alexandra. Y. (2011). 'The Grammaticalization of Evidentiality.' in Heiko Narrog and Bernd Heine (eds.), *The Oxford Handbook of Grammaticalization*, pp. 605–613. Oxford: Oxford University Press.

Aikhenvald, Alexandra. Y. (2012). 'The Essence of Mirativity.' *Linguistic Typology*. Vol.16, pp. 435–485.

Aoki, Haruo. (1986). 'Evidentials in Japanese' in Wallace Chafe and Johanna Nichols (eds.), *Evidentiality: The Linguistic Coding of Epistemology*, pp. 223–238. Norwood: Ablex.

Aoki, Hirofumi. (2007). 'Kindaigo ni okeru Jyutubu no Koozoohenka to Bunpooka (The Structural Change and Grammaticalization of the Predicates in Modern Japanese Language).' in Hirofumi Aoki. (ed.), *Nihongo no Koozoohenka to Bunpooka* (*Structral Change and Grammaticalization in Japanese Language*), pp. 205–219. Tokyo: Hituzi Syobo.

Asakawa, Tetsuya and Ayumi Takabe. (2014). *Rekisiteki Henka kara rikaisuru Gendai Nihongo Bunpoo* (*The Present-Day Japanese Grammar with Historical Insights*). Tokyo: Oufuu.

Bal, Mieke. (1985). *Narratology: Introduction to the Theory of Narrative*. Toronto: University of Toronto Press.

Barsalou, Lawrence. W. (1983). 'Ad hoc Categories.' *Memory and Cognition*, Vol.11, pp. 211–227.

Boas, Franz. (1938). 'Language.' in Franz Boas. (ed.), *General Anthropology*, pp.124–145. Boston/New York.

Brinton, Laurel and Elizabeth Closs Traugott. (2005). *Lexicalization and Language Change*. Cambridge: Cambridge University.

Bybee, Joan L., Revere Perkins, and William Pagliuca. (1994). *The Evolution of Grammar: Tense, Aspect and Modality in the Languages of the World*. Chicago: The University of Chicago Press.

Bybee, Joan L. (2011). 'Usage-Based Theory and Grammaticalization.' In Heiko Narrog and Bernd Heine (eds.), *The Oxford Handbook of Grammaticalization*, pp. 69–78. New York: Oxford University Press.

Cornillie, Bert. (2009). 'Evidentiality and Epistemic Modality. On the Close Relationship between Two Different Categories.' *Functions of Language*, Vol.16. No 1, pp. 44–62.

De Haan, Ferdinand. (1999). 'Evidentiality and Epistemic Modality: Setting Boundaries.' *Southwest Journal of Linguistics*, Vol. 18, pp. 83–101.

De Haan, Ferdinand. (2001). 'The Place of Inference within the Evidential System'. *International Journal of American Linguistics*, Vol. 67, pp. 193–219.

De Haan, Ferdinand. (2005). 'Encoding Speaker Perspective: EVIDENTIALS' *Linguistic Diversity and Language Theories*, Vol. 72, pp. 379–417. Amsterdam and Philadelphia: John Benjamins.

De Haan, Ferdinand. (2010). 'Building a Semantic Map: Top-Down versus Bottom-Up Approaches.' *Linguistic Discovery*, Vol. 8. No. 1, pp. 102–117.

DeLancey, Scott. (1997). 'Mirativity: The Grammatical Marking of Unexpected Information.' *Linguistic Typology*, Vol. 1, pp. 33–52.

DeLancey, Scott. (2001). 'The Mirative and Evidentiality.' *Journal of Pragmatics*, Vol. 33, pp. 369–382.

Genette, Gérard. (1972). *Discours du Récit, Essai de Méthode, Figures III*. Paris: Seuil. (translated by Hikaru Hanawa and Ryoichi Izumi [1985]. Tokyo: Suiseisya.)

Hamada, Hideto. (2014). 'Human Cognition and Nature of Language Diversity.' *Journal of the English Literary Society of Hakodate*, Vol. 53, pp. 1–27.

Hamada, Hideto. (2016). *Ninti to Gengo Nihongo no Sekai Eigo no Sekai (Cognition and Language:The World of Japanese and English)*. Tokyo: Kaitakusha publishing.

Hashimoto, Yosuke. (2014). *Naratorojii Nyuumon: Propp kara Genette made no Monogatariron (An Introduction to Narratology: From Propp and Genette)*. Tokyo: Suiseisya.

Hayase, Naoko. (2014). 'Kensuibunsikoobun yuraihyogen no Koobunka: Traugott and Trousdale (2013) no kanten kara (Constructionalization of the Dangling participle Construction: With Reference to Traugott and Trousdale (2013)).'in Osaka University. Graduate School of Language and Culture, *zikuu to Ninti no Gengogaku (Linguistics of space-time and Cognition)*, Vol. 4, pp. 21–30.

Heine, Bernd. and Tania Kuteva. (2007). *The Genesis of Grammar: A Reconstruction*. New York: Oxford University Press.

Honda, Akira. (2005). *Afoodansu no Nintiimiron: Seitaisinrigaku kara mita Bunpoogensyoo (Cognitive Semantics and Affordance: A Ecological Phycological Account of Linguistic Phenomenon)*. Tokyo: University of Tokyo Press.

Honda, Akira. (2013). *Tikaku to Kooi no Nintigengogaku "Watasi" wa Zibun no Soto ni aru (Perception, Action and Cogintive Lingusitics: "Watasi" as External to Oneself)*. Tokyo: Kaitakusha publishing.

Hopper, Paul. J. and Traugott, Elizabeth. Closs. (2003). *Grammaticalization*, 2nd edition. Cambridge: Cambridge University Press.

Ikegami, Yoshihiko. (2004). 'Gengo niokeru "Syukansei" to "Syukansei" no Gengoteki Sihyoo (2). (Locutionary Subjectivity and Its Linguistic Indices (2).)' *Studies in Cognitive Linguistics*, No.4, pp.1–60. Tokyo: Hituzi Syobo.

Ikegami, Yoshihiko. (2006). *Eigo no Kankaku Nihongo no Kankaku (The sense of English and the Sense of Japanese)*. Tokyo: NHK Publishing.

Ikegami, Yoshihiko. (2011). 'Nihongo no Syukansei / Syutaisei (Subjectivity in Japanese Language).' in Harumi Sawada. (ed.), *Hituzi Imiron Kooza 5 Syukansei to Syutaisei (Hituzi Semantics Study 5: Subjectivity)*, pp. 49–67. Tokyo: Hituzi Syobo.

Ikegami, Yoshihiko. (2013). '"Mie" kara "Mitate" e: "Sintaisei" / "Syukansei" ni nezasu Tatoe no Itonami no Nintigengogakuteki kiban (From "Mie" to "Mitate": A Cognitive Linguistic Account of Metaphorical Operations Rooted in Embodiment and Subjectivity).' *Papers from the National Conference of the Japanese Cognitive Linguistics Association*, Vol. 13, pp. 625–629. Japanese Cognitive Linguistics Association.

Ikegami, Yoshihiko. (2016). 'Subject-Object Contrast and Subject-Object Merger in "Thinking for Speaking."' in Kaori Kabata and Kiyoko Toratani. (eds.), *Cognitive-Functional Approaches to the Study of Japanese as a Second Language*, pp. 301–318. Boston: Mouton de Gruyter.

Iwasaki, Mariko. (2011). '"-rasi-i" no Rentaiyoohoo ni kansuru Koosatu (A Study in the Adnominal Use of "-rasi-i").' in Graduate School of Humanities and Social Sciences Okayama University, *Journal of Humanities and Social Sciences*, Vol. 32, pp. 139–158.

Iwasaki, Mariko. (2013). *Keiyoosi sei Setuzi no Imihenka ni kansuru Siteki Kenkyuu (A Historic Study in Semantic Changes of Adjective Affixes)* (Doctoral dissertation). Okayama University.

Jakobson, Roman. (1990). 'Shifters and Verbal Categories.' *On Language*, pp. 386–392, Linda R. Waugh and Monique Monville-Burston (eds). Cambridge: Harvard University.

Kamio, Akio. (1991). *Zyohoo no Nawabari Riron (The Theory of Territory of Information)*. Tokyo: Taishukan Publishing.

Kanda, Yasuko. (2005). 'Kopyura Koobun no Bunpooka — Rekisiteki Goyooron no Siten kara mita "*noda*" no Genkei Kasetu Heianki made —(A Grammaticalization of the Copula Structure: A Hypothesis of the Prototype of "-no=da" Construction From the Perspective of the Historical pragmatics).' *Bulletin of Center for Japanese Language Doshisha University*, Vol. 5, pp. 17–35. Center for Japanese Language, Doshisha University.

Kida, Kohei. (2013). 'Rasi-i to Suiron. (Rasi-i and inference.)' *The geibun-kenkyuu: Journal of Arts and Letters*, Vol 104, pp. 236–249. The Keio Society of Arts and Letter.

Kinoshita, Rika. (1998). '-*yoo=da*, -*rasi-i* — Singihandan no Modality no Taikei ni okeru "Suiron" — ("Inference" in the System of the Modality of Judgements: In the Cases of -*yoo=da* and -*rasi-i*).' *Nihongo Kyoiku (Teaching Japanese as a Foreign Language)*, Vol. 96, pp. 154–165. The Society for Teaching Japanese as a Foreign Language.

Kinoshita, Rika. (2009). 'Inga kankei no Gyaku no Seiritu to Gen'in Suiron — *Daroo* no arawasu Suironkatei — (Reasoning from Effects to Causes: Converse of the Real World Causality and -*daroo*).' *Ootemae Journal*, Vol. 9, pp. 125–136. Ootemae University.

Koyanagi, Tomokazu. (2013a). 'Kinoogo Seisan — Bunpoo Henka no Syurui I — (Grammatical Change I: The Production of Function Words).' *Inquiries into the Japanese language*, Vol. 76, pp. 60–72. Kokugakuin University Kokugo Kenkyukai.

Koyanagi, Tomokazu. (2013b). 'Bunpoo Seidoka — Bunpoo Henka no Syurui II — (Grammatical Change II: The Systemization of Grammar).' *Seisin studies*, Vol. 121, pp. 57–76. International College of the Sacred Hearts.

Langacker, Ronald. W. (1985). 'Observations and Speculations on Subjectivity.' in John Haiman. (ed.), *Iconicity in Syntax*, pp. 109–150. Amsterdam and Philadelphia: John Benjamins.

Langacker, Ronald. W. (1990). *Concept, Image, and Symbol: The Cognitive Basis of Grammar*. Cognitive Linguistics Research 1. Berlin and New York: Mouton de Gruyter.

Langacker, Ronald W. (1991). *Foundations of Cognitive Grammar, vol. 2, Descriptive Application*. Stanford: Stanford University Press.

Langacker, Ronald. W. (1999a). 'A Dynamic Usage-Based Model.' in Michael Barlow and Suzanne Kemmer. (eds.), *Usage-Based Models of Language*, pp. 1–64. Stanford, CA: CSLI.

Langacker, Ronald. W. (1999b). *Grammar and Conceptualization*. Berlin/New York:Mouton de Gruyter

Langacker, Ronald. W. (2002). 'The Control Cycle: Why Grammar is a Matter of Life and Death.' *Proceedings of the Annual Meeting of the Japanese Cognitive Linguistics Association*, Vol. 2, pp. 193–220. Japanese Cognitive Linguistics Association.

Langacker, Ronald. W. (2008). *Cognitive Grammar: A Basic Introduction*. Oxford: Oxford University Press.

Langacker, Ronald. W. (2009). *Investigation in Cognitive Grammar*. New York: Mouton de Gruyter.

Langacker, Ronald. W. (2011). 'Grammaticalization and Cognitive Grammar.' in Heiko Narrog and Bernd Heine (eds.), *The Oxford Handbook of Grammaticalization*, pp. 79–91. Oxford: Oxford University Press.

Matumura Akira. (1977). *Kindai no Kokugo: Edo kara Gendai e (Modern Japanese: From Edo Era to Contenporary Era)*. Tokyo: Ohusya.

Miyake, Tomohiro. (1994). 'Ninsikiteki Modality ni okeru Zissyooteki handan nituite (On Empirical Judgement in the Case of the Epistemic Modality).' *Kokugo Kokubun (Journal of Japanese Language and Literature)*, Vol. 63. No. 11, pp. 20–34. Kyoto University.

Miyake, Tomohiro. (2006). '"Zisshooteki handan" ga Arawasareru Syokeisiki — -*yoo=da*,-*rasi-i* o megutte — (On Forms Related to Empirical Judgement: -*yoo=da*, -*rasi-i*).' in Takashi Masuoka, Hisashi Noda, and Takuro Moriyama. (eds.), *Nihongo Bunpoo no Sintihei 2 (A New Horizon of Japanese Grammar 2)*, pp. 119–136. Tokyo: Kurosio

Publishers.
Murakami, Akiko. (1981). 'Setubizi -rasi-i no Seiritu (On the Foundations of Suffix -rasi-i).' *Kokugogaku*. Vol. 124, pp. 18–27. National Institute for Japanese Language and Linguistics.
Nakahata, Takayuki. (1992). 'Hutasikana Dentatu: -soo=da to -rasi-i (On -soo=da and -rasi-i: In Communicating Uncertainly).' *Mie Daigaku Nihon gogaku bungaku (Mie University Japanese Language and Literature)*, Vol. 3, pp. 15–24. Mie University Nihongo Bungaku Gakkai.
Nakamura, Yoshihisa. (2009). 'Nintimoodo no Syatei (The Potential of Cognitive Mode).' in Atsuro Tsubomoto, Naoko Hayase, and Naoaki Wada. (eds.), *"Uchi" to "Soto" no Gengogaku (Language and Linguistics Related to Notions of "Inside" and "outside")*, pp. 353–393. Tokyo: Kaitakusha Publishing.
Nakamura, Yoshihisa. (2012). 'Nintimoodo, Gengoruikei, Gengosinka — Saikisei (recursion) tono Kanrenkara — (Cognitive Mode, Language Types and Language Evolution: In Relation to recursion).' *Kanazawa English Studies*, Vol. 28, pp. 285–300. The Society of English Literature Kanazawa University.
Nakamura, Yoshihisa. (2016). 'Langacker no Sitenkoozu to (Kan) Syukansei — Nintibunpoo no Kizyuturyoku to Sono Kakutyoo — (The Viewing Arrangement and (Inter) Subjectivity by Langacker: Description of Cognitive Grammar and Its Extension).' in Yoshihisa Nakamura and Satoshi Uehara. (eds.), *Langacker no (Kan) Syukansei to Sono Tenkai (Langacker's (Inter)Subjectivity and Its Developments)*, pp. 1–51. Tokyo: Kaitakusha Publishing.
Nakamura, Yoshihisa. (2019). 'Ninti to Gengo, Komyunikeesyon no Sinka (The Evolution of Cognition, Language and Communication).' In: Shinya Kori and Masako Tsuzuki. (eds.), *Linguistic and Literary Analysis of Narrative: Inside/Outside Point of View*, pp. 91–120. Tokyo: Hituzi Syobo.
Nihongo Kizyutu Bunpo Kenkyukai (ed.). (2003). *Modality: Gendai Nihongo Bunpoo 4 (A Modern Japanese Grammar 4)*. Tokyo: Kuroshio Publishers.
Noya, Shigeki. (1999). *Tetugaku Kookai Nissi (A Logbook on Philosophy)*. Tokyo: Syunjuusya.
Noya, Shigeki. (2016). *Kokoro to iu Nanmon — Kuukan, Sintai, Imi (A Puzzle Called Mind: Space, Body, and Meaning)*. Tokyo: Koodansya.
Palmer, Frank. R. (1986). *Mood and Modality*. Cambridge: Cambridge University Press.
Palmer, Frank. R. (2001). *Mood and modality, 2nd edition*. Cambridge: Cambridge University Press.
Peterson, Tyler. (2017). 'Problematizing Mirativity.' *Review of Cognitive Linguistics*. Vol 15, Issue 2, pp.312–342. The Auspices of the Spanish Cognitive Linguistics Association.
Quirk, Randolph, Sidney Greenbaum, Geoffrey Leech, and Jan Svartvik. (1985). *A Comprehensive Grammar of the English Language*. London: Pearson Longman.
Radden, Günter and René Dirven. (2007). *Cognitive English Grammar*. Amsterdam and Philadelphia: John Benjamins.
Sadanobu, Toshiyuki. (2008). *Bon'noo no Bunpoo — Taiken o Kataritagaru Hitobito no Yokuboo ga Nihongo no Bunpoo Sisutemu o Yusaburu Hanasi (Grammar and the Earthly Desires: How People Undermine the Japanese Grammar System by Fulfilling Their Desires to Talk About Their Own Experiences)*. Tokyo: Chikuma Syoboo.
Senba, Mituaki. (1972). 'Syuusi-rentaikei setuzoku no '-gena' to '-souna'. (A Study of '-gena' and '-souna' followed by ending/attributive forms.)' *Kokugogaku Ronsyuu: Saeki Umetomo Hakusi Kizyu Kinen*, pp. 513–535. Tokyo: Hyogensya.
Suzuki, Hideaki. (1988). 'Meijiki ikoo no -rasi-i no Henboo (On Change of -rasi-i from the Meiji Period Onward).' *Kokugo Kokubun (Journal of Japanese Language and Literature)*, Vol. 57. No. 3, pp. 42–59. Kyoto University.

Sweetser, Eve. (1990). *From Etymology to Pragmatics: Metaphorical and Cultural Aspects of Semantic Structure*. Cambridge: Cambridge University Press.
Takashima, Akira. (2018). 'Syookosei "-rasi-i" no Bunpoka o Dookizukeru Datusyutaika no Purosesu (On the Process of De-Subjectification Affecting Grammaticalization of Evidential *-rasi-i*).' in Nakamura Yoshihisa Kyoozyu Taisyoku Kinen Ronbunsyuu Kankokai. (eds.), *Kotoba no Perspective (Perspectives on Language)*, pp. 417–428. Tokyo: Kaitakusha Publishing.
Takashima, Akira. (2019). 'Syookosei "-rasi-i" no Mirative eno Kakutyoo (An analysis of the extension of meaning into mirativity in the Japanese evidential marker *-rasi-i*).' *Papers from the National Conference of the Japanese Cognitive Linguistics Association*, Vol. 19, pp. 298–310. Japanese Cognitive Linguistics Association.
Takashima, Akira. (2020a). 'Syoosetu ni okeru Nihongo to Eigo no Syookosei ni tuite (On Evidentiality in Japanese and English Observed in Novels).' *Journal of the English Literary Society of Hakodate*, Vol. 59, pp. 69–84.
Takashima, Akira. (2020b). 'Syutaisei to Datusyutaisei ni kannsite — Syookosei "-rasi-i" no Bunpooka (On Subjectification and De-Subjectification: Grammaticalization of *-rasi-i*).' *Human and Socio-Environmental Studies*, Vol. 40, pp. 101–115. Graduate School of Human and Socio-Environmental Studies Kanazawa University.
Takashima, Akira. (2021). *A Cognitive Approach to Evidentiality — A Case of Evidential -rasi-i in Japanese-*. (Doctoral dissertation), Kanazawa University.
Takashima, Akira. (2022). 'A Study on the Relationship between Inference and Metaphor.' *Journal of the English Literary Society of Hakodate*, Vol. 61, pp. 19–34.
Takeda, Seiji. (2005[1989]). *Gensyoogaku Nyuumon (An Introduction to Phenomelogy)*. Tokyo: NHK Publishing.
Teramura, Hideo. (1984). *Nihongo no Syntax to Imi II (Japanese Syntax and Meaning II)*. Tokyo: Kuroshio Publishers.
Tomasello, M. (1999). *The cultural origins of human cognition*. Harvard University Press.
Tomasello, M. (2003). *Constructing a language: A usage-based theory of language acquisition*. Cambridge, MA: Harvard University Press.
Traugott, Elizabeth Closs. (2010a). '(Inter)Subjectivity and (Inter)Subjectification: A Reassessment.' in Kristin Davidse, Lieven Vandelanotte, and Hurbert Cuyckens. (eds.), *Subjectification, Intersubjectification and Grammaticalization*, pp. 29–74. Berlin/New York: Walter de Gruyter.
Traugott, Elizabeth Closs. (2010b). 'Grammaticalization.' In: Silvia Luraghi and Vit Bubenik (eds.), *Continuum Companion to Historical Linguistics*, pp. 269–283. London: Continuum Press.
Yamamoto, Sawako. (2012). 'Modality Keisiki "-rasi-i" no Seiritu (The Foundation of *-rasi-i* as a Modality Form).' in Yoshiyuki Takayama, Hiroshi Aoki, and Yoshiichiro Fukuda. (eds.), *Nihongo Bunpoosi Kenkyuu 1 (A Historical Study of Japanese Grammar 1)*, pp. 165–188. Tokyo: Hituzi Syobo.
Yoshida, Kanehiko. (1971). *Gendai Zyodoosi no Siteki Kenkyuu (A Diachronic Study in Modern Auxiliary Verbs)*. Tokyo: Meiji Syoin.
Yonekura, Yoko. (2013). 'Ruizisei kara Hasseisuru (Kan) Syukanteki Yoohoo — Tyokuyu kara Inyoo doonyuukinoo e no Bunpooka — ((Inter) Subjectification Usages Produced by the Process of Analogy: On the Grammaticalization from Simile to the Function of Introducing Quotations).' in Masaaki Yamanashi, Kimihiro Yoshimura, Kaoru Horie, and Yosuke Momiyama. (eds.), *Ninti Rekisi Gengogaku (Historical Cognitive Linguistics)*, pp. 137–164. Tokyo: Kuroshio Publishers.
Yuzawa, Kokichiro. (1955). *Tokugawa Zidai Gengo no Kenkyuu (A study in Languages in*

the Tokugawa Period). Tokyo: Kazama Syobo.

Yonemori, Yuji. (2007). *Abduction — Kasetu to Hakken no Ronri (The Logic of Assumptions and Discoveries)*. Tokyo: Keiso Syobo.

Van der Auwera, Joan. and Plungian, Vladimir. A. (1998). 'Modality's semantic map.' *Linguistic Typology*, Vol. 2, pp. 79–124. Berlin/New York: De Gruyter Mouton.

Whorf, B. L. (1956 [2012]). *Language, Thought, and Reality (Selected Writings of Benjamin Lee Whorf)*. John B. Carroll. (eds.), Cambridge, Massachusetts; London, England: MIT Press.

Data Sources

Arishima, Takeo. (1950). *Aru Onna*. Aozora Bunko.
Brown, Dan. (2017). *Origin*. New York: Knopf Doubleday Publishing Group. (Echizen, Toshiya (trans.). [2018]. *Origin*. Tokyo: Kadokawa Bunko.)
Cranston, Edin. A. (1998). *A Waka Anthology*. Vol. 1. Stanford: Stanford University Press.
Isaka, Kotaro. (2008). *Sinigami no Seido*. Tokyo: Bunsyun Bunko.
Ishiguro, Kazuo. (2015). *The Buried Giant*. New York: Knopf Doubleday Publishing Group. (Tuchiya, Masao (trans.). [2015]. *Wasurerareta Kyozin*. Tokyo: Hayakawa Shobo.)
Kirn, Walter. (2001). *Up in the Air*. London: John Murray. (Eguchi, Taiko (trans.). [2010]. *Myrage, Mylife*. Tokyo: Shogakkan.)
Kabuki Daityo Kenkyukai (ed). (1984). *Kabuki Daityoo Syusei*, Vol.4. Tokyo: Benseisya.
Kagiwara Masaaki (ed). (2000). *Gikeiki*. Nihon Koten Bungaku Taikei, Vol.62. Tokyo: Syogakkan.
Kawabata, Yasunari. (2019). *Koto*. Tokyo: Shincyo Bunko.(Holman, J. Martin (trans.). [1987]. *The Old Capital*. Tokyo/Rutland/Singapore: Tuttle Publishing.)
Kawateke Sigetosi (ed). (1920). *Mokuami Kyakuhonsyuu*, Vol.5. Tokyo: Syunyodo.
Koda Rohan. (1978). 'Kooinga.' *Rohan Zensyuu*, Vol.1. Kagyukai (ed). Tokyo: Iwanami Syoten.
Koda Rohan. (1978). 'Kiku-no Hamamatu.' *Rohan Zensyuu*, Vol.8. Kagyukai (ed). Tokyo: Iwanami Syoten.
Kokusyo Kankokai (ed). (1915). *Tokugawa Bungei Ruijyu*, Vol.7. Tokyo: Kokusyo Kankôkai.
Kono Toshiro and Momoko Hirotu (eds). (1982). *Teihon Hirotu Ryuuroo Sakuhinsyuu Ge*. Hirosima: Tokasya.
Mori, Ogai. (1948). *Seinen*. Aozora Bunko.
Minato, Kanae. (2008). *Kokuhaku*. Tokyo: Futabasha. (Snyder, Stephen (trans.). [2014]. *Confessions*. New York: Mulholland Books.)
Murakami, Haruki. (1982). *Hituji wo Meguru Booken*. Tokyo: Kodansha.(Birnbaum, Alfred (trans.). [2000]. *A Wild Sheep Chase*. London: Vintage Books.)
Murakami, Haruki. (2014). *Onna no Inai Otokotati*. Tokyo: Bungeisyunjyuu.
Muto Sadao and Masahiko Oka(eds). (1976). *Hanasibon Taikei*, Vol.4. Tokyo: Tokyodo Syuppan.
Nakamura, Fuminori. (2013). *Suri*. Tokyo: Kawade Bunko. (Izumo, Satoko and Coates, Stephen (trans.). [2012]. *The Thief*. London: Corsair.)
National Institute for Japanese Language and Linguistics. *The Balanced Corpus of Contemporary Written Japanese (BCCWJ)*.
Ozaki, Koyo. (1969). *Konzikiyasya*. Tokyo: Shincyo Bunko.(Lloyd, Arthur. M (trans.). [1917]. *The Golden Demon*. Tokyo: Seibundo.
Sigetomo Ki (ed). (1958). *Tikamatu Jyorurisyuu Jyo*. Nihon Koten Bungaku Taikei, Vol.49. Tokyo: Iwanami Syoten.
Tezuka Osamu. (1993). *Black Jack*. Tokyo: Akita Bunko.(Nieh, Camellia (trans.). [2008]. *Black Jack*. New York: Vertical.)
Tukamoto Tetuzo and Sigeki Minami (eds). (1922). *Kyakuhonsyuu Ge*. Tokyo: Ariakedo Syoten.
Urayama Masao and Hitosi Matuzaki (eds). (1960). *Kabuki kyakuhonsyuu jyo*. Nihon Koten Bungaku Taikei, Vol. 53. Tokyo: Iwanami Syoten.
Waley Arthur and Dennis Washburn (trans). (2010). *The Tale of Genji*. Tokyo: Tuttle Publishing.

Index

A
affordance theory   120

C
clausal grounding   40
clausal-internal grounding system   42
clause-external grounding elements   42
clause-internal grounding elements   41
cognitive grammar (CG)   1, 35
control cycle   41
cycle of awakening   50, 121

D
de-subjectification   46
D-mode   46

E
embodied cognition   45
epistemic assessment   27
epistemic modality   17, 23
evidential marker -*rasi-i*   2, 54
evidential modality   15, 16
evidential -*rasi i*   16, 78, 88, 91, 97, 105
evidentiality   1, 5, 7, 15, 23
evidentiality strategies   13, 22

F
fashion of construal   101, 102
focalization   99, 100, 107
first-person effect   29, 113
functionalization   70

G
grammaticalization   21, 64
ground   35
Grounding   39
grounding elements   40

H
hearsay   2, 9, 12, 15, 19, 20, 56
hearsay parameter   93

I
immediate scope   36
I-mode   46
inference   2, 9, 15, 56
inference parameter   9, 91

L
layered structure   43, 93

M
maximal scope   36
mirativity   29, 30
mode of cognition   46, 118

N
narratology   98
nominal grounding   40

O
objective construal   103

R
reduction model of grammaticalization   69
reported parameters   9

S
Sapir-Whorf hypothesis   101
sensory parameters   8
subjectification   37, 38, 39
subjective construal   103
subjectivity   35
suffix -*rasi-i*   76, 87, 91
suffixal usage of -*rasi-i*   2, 54, 55

T

theory of territory   115

V

viewing arrangement   35, 46

髙島彬（たかしま あきら）

略歴
尾道市立大学芸術文化学部日本文学科講師（言語学担当）。金沢大学大学院で認知言語学を学び、2021年に博士課程修了、博士号（文学）取得。現在、言語類型論や証拠性、日本語と英語を対象とした比較対照分析を中心に研究。

Akira Takashima is a Lecturer in the Department of Japanese Literature, the Faculty of Art and Culture, Onomichi City University, Japan. He obtained a PhD in Literature from Kanazawa University in 2021, specializing in cognitive linguistics. His current research interests include linguistic typology, evidentiality and contrastive studies of Japanese and English expressions.

主な論文
・「日本語と英語における証拠性「推量」の使用の揺れについて」『JELS 42』（2025）
・「現代日本語「〜感」に反映されるFictive Interaction」『日本認知言語学会論文集23』（2023）
・「証拠性「らしい」のミラティブへの拡張」『日本認知言語学会論文集19』（2019）

Hituzi Linguistics in English No.40
Evidentiality in Japanese
A Cognitive Linguistic Approach to the Evidential Marker -rasi-i

発行	2025年3月14日 初版1刷
定価	11000円＋税
著者	©髙島彬
発行者	松本功
ブックデザイン	白井敬尚形成事務所
印刷・製本所	亜細亜印刷株式会社
発行所	株式会社 ひつじ書房

〒112-0011 東京都文京区千石2-1-2 大和ビル2F
Tel: 03-5319-4916
Fax: 03-5319-4917
郵便振替00120-8-142852
toiawase@hituzi.co.jp
https://www.hituzi.co.jp/
ISBN978-4-8234-1278-3

造本には充分注意しておりますが、落丁・乱丁などがございましたら、小社かお買上げ書店にておとりかえいたします。ご意見、ご感想など、小社までお寄せ下されば幸いです。

刊行のご案内

Hituzi Linguistics in English

No. 36 Integrated Skills Development
Comprehending and Producing Texts in a Foreign Language
中森誉之 著　定価 11,000 円＋税

No. 37 Perception and Linguistic Form
A Cognitive Linguistic Analysis of the Copulative Perception Verb Construction
徳山聖美 著　定価 11,000 円＋税

No. 38 The *No More A than B* Construction
A Cognitive and Pragmatic Approach
廣田篤 著　定価 12,000 円＋税

No. 39 A Contrastive Study of Function in Intonation Systems
角岡賢一 著　定価 8,000 円＋税